ECKO

ECKO

FIRED FOR SUCCESS?

TRUE STORIES AND MANAGEMENT LESSONS
FOR OUR TOUGH CHANGING TIMES

BY

KURT GASSNER

My-mindguide.com

Ecko
Kurt Gassner

Impressum
My-mindguide – The publishing trademarke of trendguide Capital GmbH, Klenzestr. 42a, 80469 Munich, Germany.

Reg. Nr. HRB Munich 206639, VAT 152 123 159, CEO: Kurt Friedrich Gassner
Web: www.my-mindguide.com, mail: gassner@my-mindguide.com

Paperback ISBN: 978-3-949978-82-1
Hardback ISBN: 978-3-949978-83-8

Table of Contents

Preface

Ecko, the first Multi-media Mailorder company was fired for success (it threatended the classical book-club Business.

It took Amazon more than 12 years to prove that its business was profitable. This is a true-life story about the failure culture in today's management.

ECCO had a bright future ahead of them as the first online and offline book merchandise seller globally. It's the year 1989. The German Bücherbund, a part of the Holtzbrinck Group in Germany, looked for a new business model because the old business model was outdated.

More than two million book club subscribers had been obliged to buy four books a year. They were also offered a 5th book for Christmas, and it was like a money machine. Can you imagine that two million people buy books each quarter? Most books are promoted, so it costs less money to produce them. It has become expensive to get new subscribers. New subscribers mean spending more money. The costs were skyrocketing, and for the management, it was logical that the business model was outdated.

Mr. Unkelbach, the CEO, and Mr. Gruenberg, the Head of Marketing, collaborated on catalog and promotion ideas this time. I worked for Deutsche Bücherbund as an ad agency, and we came up with ideas to revolutionize the business model.

We found a new model that was better than the old one. The idea was to entertainingly sell books, media, and other goods per mail order. It was not easy to convince the very conservative Holtzbrinck group. After much thought, they sold the whole company to the Kirch Group, the biggest movie and licensing company in Europe at that time.

The Kirch Group was interested in the concept of the company. A pitch was set between Springer & Jacobi, a high-ranked star agency in Hamburg, and me—with a middle-sized agency in Munich. Surprisingly, we won. That was only the beginning.

I hired a first-class team: Dhalan Netch, a Creative Director from NY, and Prof. Anton Mayr (later the Dean of Marketing at the University of Munich), a Marketing Professor. I also hired many people from overseas, including art directors from London. We bought the first Apple computers directly from the US and imported them. We even had to change the power system to adapt it to 220V.

Mr. Gruenberg also set up a completely new, highly motivated team of buyers and specialists on the client-side. It was so strange that the old, conservative Buecherbund was working day and night with the startup guys in jeans and sneakers. (The term "startup" had not been invented).

We invented ECKO, the first mail-order company that sold books, videos, and all types of media, some of which you can still find on Amazon. We started with service, great enthusiasm, and a campaign and catalog that rocked.

Unbelievably, orders flooded in by the millions. We sold a piece of the Berlin Wall. We had significant investments in infrastructure, stock, and mail, and after a year, sales were increasing, but the business was still not profitable.

We decided to try something different. Mr. Gruenberg and I created an entirely new culture. We had weekend retreats to form team spirit. There was no difference between clients and agencies anymore. The whole team had one goal and one energy level. It was suspicious, and the conservative management had a sharp eye on us.

But it worked.

Nobody focused on time.

Some weekend offices were crowded. We worked till late at night.

That was the start of the breakthrough.

In 1990, ECCO, the new shark in mail order, was the talk of the book and media business world. At the most significant direct marketing fair, ECCO was the talk of the day. Everyone was astounded by the progress. We won thousands of new customers each month outside of the club world. Everything was going along fine, and the whole team was highly motivated.

Then it happened.

In 1991, the Deutsche Bücherbund was sold to Bertelsmann, the biggest competitor and running the most substantial club business in Europe. After the sale, we presented the perspectives of ECKO.

We had many regular buying customers, and we argued that this would be the lifeline for the whole book-club business.

We pointed out that we had started to operate with BTX, a mix between phone and TV, to place orders.

Also, we predicted that BTX or a similar electronic device would take over the world and revolutionize the world of marketing shortly. (In CERN, Geneve, the first website was created in 91).

No, we didn't have a clue how exactly it would happen.

We imagined some electronic interaction system; we read about the first website at CERN, Geneve, in 1990 and the first web server.

We thought we were close to a revolution in the world of mail-order, and that would make a big difference.

We also had the vision of selling this model globally.

Yes, we had big dreams and also a clear vision.

Mr. Gruenberg, my team, and I worked like hell.

I worked on the creative part while he crunched the numbers.

But no, they decided to sell ECKO, the innovation pearl, to a publishing company named WELTBILD, owned by the German Catholic church in 1991.

ECKO was a side business for them at the time, the unliked stepdaughter (not invented by us).

It soon disappeared from the market.

A great future was lost.

Weltbild also ran out of business a couple of years later.

It was a disaster for all of us.

Hundreds of people were sacked.

I had to fire more than forty employees.

Mr. Gruenberg started a big lottery business and won a fortune.

My Creative Director, Dhalan Netch, went back to Miami, and we partnered with an ad agency based in the US.

I also started new ventures in Germany and Austria.

Many people still remember the glorious days of ECKO, the natural origin of Amazon.

We had a diverse, multiracial, and multi-cultural team from the client's and the agency side.

An absolute novelty in these times in Germany. I had set up an international team of thirty creative cracks from all over the world, now based in Munich.

We worked on a new culture and a new ECKO mindset.

What would have happened if the Bertelsmann management had decided differently?

ECKO was close to profitability in the second year with the classical mail order business.

 Its vision was to be the first website with a database of two million buying customers.

ECKO was ready to go global because we had a multiracial, international team.

The argument was that "we don't want to cannibalize our club business."

"We believe in our book-club business!" (it is and was always our cash cow)

That crazy business model with selling books on phones, mail-order, electronic devices is not in our strategic interest, and your fantasies about future electronic order systems for the public are pure science fiction.

How crazy!

They thought the world would be fine if they monopolized the book club business.

They bought Buecherbund for the book club business and eliminated their strategic competitor.

This decision follows a pattern very often seen even in today's big companies.

Monopolize, reduce costs and competition, block new ventures, never risk, and never change the company culture.

It's risky.
This decision was a multi-billion disaster.

Today, the value of Amazon is roughly 100 times greater than the value of Bertelsmann.

What happened to the decision-makers?

They were all rewarded with bonuses and fat pensions because part of the management culture in Europe is that if you make it into the decision-maker club (CEO or similar), you stay there for your lifetime. (You have to steal the golden spoon to be fired)

Today, the book club business is dead. Amen. RIP.

Amazon made it with a concept similar to ECKO: lots of services, easy transactions, global thinking, no strings attached, etc.

Just as we predicted, in 1990/91, the internet was founded.

In 1993, the first websites went public, and in July 1994, Jeff Bezos opened his business in a garage and founded Amazon.

This was a complex reality to face.

Other individuals, I feel, fail because they have no idea what they're doing. They're losers who have no business in that line of work. I was under the impression that this didn't apply to me or our idea, especially since we'd had previous successes: "I've come out on top." I had previously been successful. I'll be successful once more. Keep an eye on me!

Failure was something that only other people were affected by. That was my mentality at the time. As a result, I thought I had good reason to be arrogant. I had a long string of victories with only a few minor setbacks to show for it.

The Beast of Failure coiled its tentacles around me and bit me in the ass just as I had achieved new heights of confidence and bravado. My knowledgeable, professional, and well-prepared ass got a good, hard-to-ignore, and impossible-to-forget bite.

I had the option of licking my wounds or biting back. I decided to bite back.

Failure became my arch-enemy.

Defeating it is my obsession, and teaching others how to beat it is my mission.

This book is part of that mission.

Why this book?

This book is intended to be an outlier within management and leadership. I believe this is necessary if society cultivates better and wiser leaders.

The remaining chapters explore the most common leadership styles.

Groups also make mistakes at the organizational, managerial, team, and individual levels. But before we delve in, it's important to note that not all leaders' mistakes are created equally.

There are small, inconsequential challenges that have little effect on a leader's career, and then there are the big ones, the high-visibility, devastating challenges that can destroy careers. And the higher you go in an organization, the bigger the mistakes can become.

Consider the comparison of rock climbing. Like starting business leaders, beginning rock climbers focus on skill development and technique. They practice knot tying. Scrapes and bruises are the results of mistakes. Even a long fall is almost always recoverable, albeit potentially more severe—teams, or "ropes," form as climbers progress. Climbers now rely on one another to stay alive. A single misplaced piton could lead to a team member's death.

Finally, the rope team's leader gains even more specialized skills.

Rope leaders can establish an identifiable "sense of path" up a mountain via experience—trial and error. To the untrained eye, this sense of direction may appear instinctive. Still, experienced climbers understand that it is the result of wisdom gained via a series of successes and, more importantly, crucial lessons acquired from failures. The rope leader ensures that the purpose and progress (the route to the top) are clear and attainable. The entire crew could perish if the rope leader makes a mistake.

In business, the same relationships exist. Like young rock climbers, many young leaders are consumed with attaining technical skills. Their resource responsibility is usually limited, and so is the impact of their actions beyond their success or failure. One end of the spectrum is where senior-level leaders have more responsibility and can do more. This means that their mistakes are magnified, even multiplied.

ECCO

14-TAGE RÜCKGABERECHT
Paßt nicht? Zurück-
schicken! Bei ECCO haben
Sie die Hosen an.
ECCO will zufriedene Kunden. Deshalb haben Sie 14 Tage lang volles Rückgaberecht (Musik & Video bitte nur original verpackt), falls mal etwas nicht Ihren Erwartungen entspricht. Agal, aus welchem Grund. Unsers Devise: Über Geschmack läßt sich streiten, über guten Kundendienst nicht.
DIE TOTEN HOSEN
1000 GUTE GRÜNDE
ECCO
DER BUCH, MUSIK UND VIDEO EXPRESS

My-mindguide.com

The failure paradox

Failure and defeat are life's most outstanding teachers.

While every great leader makes mistakes, there is a limit to how many mistakes you can make before demonstrating yourself unworthy of leadership—you can only tumble from the corporate ladder so many times before your climb is over. And the higher you climb, the worse the fall will be; failure will become inconceivable. This is when the downward spiral of "winning at all costs" can start, even if it involves hiding mistakes, blaming subordinates, or even lying. Simply put, failing is not an option at a certain level. However, to achieve success, we must be familiar with failure. This is what the failure paradox is all about.

In this book, we will talk frankly and instructively about the things that are hard to talk about.

There is a solution, and it is right in front of our eyes. True, we all make errors, but hopefully, we'll learn from them. But the genuine opportunity comes when we can learn from other people's failures before we face similar issues ourselves; we can absorb the lessons without paying the price. And this point of view is beginning to acquire traction.

There is a growing understanding that what makes leaders effective is their ability to learn from mistakes, both their own and others.

How much do we talk about learning from failure? How much about learning from success? The gap between them is growing, suggesting we prefer to learn from flops.

The entire experience with ECKO made me think twice. Because we've all been raised differently and because most of us have been punished for making errors in the past, I had never been able to say to my company's diverse workforce, "Have no fear of failure!" and expect it to be true right away. (I used to think I could manage people like that, but now I know better). Today, I see that influential business leaders and coaches must create stories that celebrate failure and incredible learning opportunities. Then they must tell those stories repeatedly until their employees understand and believe them.

The goal is often to change a lifetime of learned responses that failure is wrong and that you will be shouted at, warned, or even physically threatened, punished, or fired on the spot if you fail so that you don't think that way.

So, I will keep repeating my chant to persuade people to share my conviction in failure's greatness. Because I think that failing is not only acceptable but necessary, my teammates must fight to overcome their fears of failing and blunders. You will not be punished for failing.

After more than 40 years in business, I am sure that the shortest path to success is to have a "no fear" attitude toward failure. Leaders and front-line workers must put their necks out a mile every day to do their jobs well, be successful, and keep their companies competitive. They must produce risky, cutting-edge, game-changing ideas, plans, presentations, advice, technology, products, leadership, and bills, among other things. And they have to do it all without fear of failure, rejection, or punishment.

Leaders and managers must encourage risk and accept failure to achieve this. For many, doing so will be a leap of faith until they have firsthand experience with the rewards of failing. Until then, I hope these stories of my spectacular failures, as well as the lessons my teammates, business, and I have gained from them, will motivate you to "celebrate failure."

Managers are people like you.

If humans have changed enormously, managers can change too. Their expectations and demands of their managers can change as well. It is the company that has not followed the change in mentalities. People today are not the same as 20 years ago. They no longer say "I belong" to such a company. There is a lot of "turnover," permanent arrivals, and departures, including in the "best" structures. Today, working people are no longer afraid to leave or resign because they are not fulfilled.

Why can't managers do the same?
There is always a human at the forefront of the qualities required.

A human with flaws and weaknesses.
The pressure to keep everything in order is more significant for leadership, often encouraging behaviors that ignore caring for their mental health. Without time for self-care, managers

turn to watch for employees and the company's operational processes.

A manager has different responsibilities within a company. In addition to ensuring the teams' productivity, this professional needs to mediate conflicts, offer support for the development of the work, correct deficits and weak points, and, above all, build trust among the team.

While they are rewarding, senior management positions are more likely to suffer from excess stress. At the same time, the manager must deal with pressure, demand for results, and increased responsibility. This, in turn, is the source of multiple health problems.

Managers fear that their weaknesses are justifications for their inability to hold a leadership position. In this way, in an attempt to demonstrate efficiency and for fear of taking their emotional problems to HR, leaders end up neglecting themselves.

Fear of being human

Fear is a universal human problem. We are all afraid of something, and managers are too scared, no matter how hard they try to convince us otherwise. Thinking about human leadership, many top managers who have always tried to be heroes throughout their careers feel like the ground is slipping from under their feet. One CEO recently confided to me, "I was taught never to show emotion or vulnerability at work." And you say that it is necessary. This is a real revolution." The fear of such managers is usually expressed in one of the following three forms:

Fear of contact with one's own emotions

Looking inward is difficult and even dangerous for a rational manager who relies on analytical skills. What will they find there? Self-analysis can confuse all the cards. Even more frightening is that the manifestation of the actual "I" can break their external image. Do they suddenly seem weak? What if they lose control, authority, respect, or love?

Fear of chaos

Many leaders think that if all employees treat each other as individuals, they will start hugging and singing songs instead of working. One top manager even told me, "The office is not a place for emotions." How will the leader manage the company if they no longer have to solve all the problems? What happens when they relinquish control? With this thought, many of my clients feel like circus performers without a safety net.

Fear of failure

Many leaders don't know what to do with emotions at work, both their own and those of others. One client asked me, "What if my employee tells me they lost a parent or spouse due to COVID-19? What if someone cries? I have no idea what to do or what to say then!" Effectively leading the heart and soul requires skills and abilities that leaders accustomed to working using their left hemisphere and good judgment do not yet have. Worse, these leaders are used to being successful, but they become afraid of catastrophic failures in such cases. One senior executive told me, "I was a good, old-fashioned leader." And I like the idea of becoming a new type of leader. But can I achieve the same success?

Many managers wonder how they can become human leaders.

Before leaders, however, the professionals who occupy this position are human beings. They feel just like everyone else.

Why, then, do they go to such lengths to hide this obvious side of their existence?

There has to be a better way.

Because the question of "why" is not asked enough! The problem is that the business world is constantly looking for itself; the old model is very difficult to leave. It is still very present because organizations are afraid to part with their culture.

We often point the finger at managers, pointing them out as responsible for all the evils. What do you think?

The fear of becoming a human manager stems from old beliefs and expectations. I will call them "mindset traps." We all carry many different voices that determine how we view ourselves, others, the world, and our behavior. Sometimes these are other people's voices, such as the voices of our parents or teachers, and sometimes they are collective beliefs, stereotypes, and standards from our environment, in particular, social and religious values. These voices shape our worldview, and, in some cases, when they are linked to traumatic events, they can even change the shape of our brains.

I meet many managers, and I can assure you that they are rarely idiots or imbeciles! They often want to do well, but they are drowned in loops and "processes" beyond them.

Everyone runs in all directions without really knowing why.

Almost all of us suffer from the same mental traps, visible or invisible, that hold us back and make us afraid of change—but we can get rid of them.

What's next?

Getting rid of the traps of thinking requires courage: the courage to change old beliefs, to listen to yourself and not to other people's voices, to question what we used to think is right, to cope with the fear of the unknown. You can only change your mindset if you feel fear and act anyway. In this case, we can change our point of view, free ourselves from delusions, and become human managers.

By recognizing your thinking pitfalls, you must build and reinforce a new point of view that will be more useful to you. Create a new mental construct. To do this, you first need to freely imagine who you could become and then put these ideas into practice. This unique point of view must be deeply rooted so that you do not fall back into old habits of thought and action. It needs to be incorporated into your life and your leadership. To embrace a new way of thinking, living, and acting requires learning and practice.

Human managers have a profound impact on the lives of their loved ones, their companies, and the world. The path from the mind trap to the mind construct separates the past managers from those who will successfully meet the present and future challenges. You, too, can become a human manager and brighten our world with your light.

PART 1
START

ECCO

Kein Club. Kein Kauf-
zwang. Kein Rechnung
ohne den Wirt.

Regelmäßige Kaufverpflichtungen
können ganz schön lästig werden. Schon
mancher hat festgestellt, daß ihm der
Spaß da schnell vergeht. ECCO ver-
pflichtet Sie zu nichts. Bei uns ent-
scheiden Sie, ob Sie bestellen oder nicht.
Denn wir wollen nur zufriedene Kunden.
Und dazu brauchen
Sie keinen Mit-
gliedsausweis.

ECCO

My-mindguide.com

Chapter 1

FLAWED MANAGEMENT

Special committees, strategic projects, boards of directors, and business volunteering are all management. There are many ways to seek out new skills, demonstrate leadership and promote professional growth. However, it is crucial to continue to perform its current functions well.

Ideally, our mandates include challenges to surpass ourselves and show our abilities. This will score points with the management. But the orders must be attainable. Don't try to jump five steps at a time because the risk of failure would be too significant.

They sometimes say that it is lonely at the top. As a manager, you will notice that there is always an invisible barrier between you and your employees. No matter how informal you are with your employees, they will always consider you the boss.

When you're in a managerial position, you cannot always be a friend to everyone. How would you like to sue someone if they are not functioning correctly? Or worse, to tell an employee that they no longer have a job?

A higher position does not only mean that you can delegate more. You are also responsible for the functioning of others. So, you will occasionally have to take the proverbial beating for the evil work of someone else. Count on your workload increasing, and you will have to work longer working days.

What if we fail? Failure is not fatal. It is an attitude that can be the worst reaction, the one that could put the brakes on your career? Blaming everyone and all sorts of factors. You have to assume what happens, try to understand the reasons for your failure, and bounce back quickly.

That's what a good manager does.

Becoming A Manager

Do you think you can deal with the flaws, and do you still want to become a manager? That's nice, but of course, you haven't gotten there yet.

You need an aptitude for it to fulfill a role as a manager. Your superiors must see that you have that aptitude to get the position. You must also know your field, and you must also showcase this.

So, the first step to becoming a manager in the company you work for is to put yourself in good light with the people who can help you in the saddle. This generally means that you will have to do more work, work overtime more often, and help current managers do their job. Just saying you could do better isn't enough.

Skills

You don't have to be an expert and have read all the management books to become a manager. However, there are several skills you should have or develop:

- **Communication:** Employees below you, your co-managers, and your superiors: when you are in control, quite a few people want to talk to you. Be careful when you have something to say; don't discredit yourself by setting expectations too high. Do not always speak for yourself; you must also be a good listener.

- **Persuasion:** You will have to convince people to do what you want from day one. Whether you want your employees to show more commitment or pull a bigger budget from the board, you will have to get them to get your way.

- **Leadership is a difficult quality to cultivate because it is often based on the respect and trust of those around you.** In a nutshell, you have to be charismatic enough to let people follow you blindly if you want to go in a specific direction, even if that means making sacrifices together.

Questions to Ask

1. What attracts me most in a management position?

Strong managers take responsibility—both for the work of the team members and for everyone's well-being in the workplace. Do power and authority particularly stimulate you? Then you put your image on the line, and you won't get very far in your career.

2. Do I have the motivation?

Motivated managers have ambition. They want to exert their influence within the company. They know what drives them and have the inner strength to stay motivated and inspire others.

3. How do I interact with others?

Managers communicate to inspire. They boost the morale of the people around them. Do you like talking to people? Do you notice that your colleagues take your ideas and advice to heart?

If you are more withdrawn, then management is probably not for you.

4. Do I like to take on a new challenge?

Managers want to develop themselves. They learn from mistakes made and successes achieved. And above all, they are constantly raising the bar and looking for new challenges. You are doomed to fail as a manager if you and your team keep making the same mistakes or avoiding new challenges.

5. Do I have confidence in myself?

Successful managers have a strong belief in their abilities without appearing arrogant. Do you strike the right balance between taking charge and delegating authority?

6. Can I adapt well?

Nothing is black and white. Good managers mainly see the shades of gray. Your feelings and views are not sacred. Pay attention to the nuances. Adapt to the diverse personalities and working methods of your team.

7. Do I take time for others?

A manager takes the time to manage others and answer questions. At the same time, you have to get your work done. Before you are a leader, success is all about growing yourself. When you become a leader, success is all about growing others.

8. Am I open to constructive criticism?

Tall trees catch a lot of wind. Strong managers are not shaken by criticism. On the contrary, they see it as an opportunity to learn. It is not a given for everyone to not take criticism too personally. You can learn it with time.

9. Can I handle the confrontation?

Intense discussions are part of the job. Managers don't shy away from them, even if they upset former colleagues or work friends. Are you able to reprimand or even fire famous employees for not performing?

10. Do I take responsibility?

Successful managers feel responsible not only for their work but also for the performance of their team members. When someone on your team makes a wrong turn, it reflects your leadership. Learning to deal with this is a difficult adjustment.

Did you answer "yes" to most of those questions? Fantastic! You have the strength and motivation to go far in a management position. Did you reply "no" more often? That's also okay! Many people feel pressured to take on management jobs. But is that what you want? You can also excel and grow without taking charge.

The Performance Review Trap

Performance reviews are a very commonly (mis)used tool in organizations.

Competencies: A Changing State or A Personality Trait?
Before creating an assessment, it is essential to know whether you are trying to measure a state or a personality trait to know the best method to use.

A state is something that varies over time. Example: emotion, skill, or knowledge.

However, personality traits can have more stable patterns. For example, more introverted people vs. more extroverted people.

A simple competence assessment does not make sense for this second group. Personality tests are used to create a self-assessment on top of carefully elaborated sentences or situational judgment tests. And yet it is questionable.

If we want to measure something abstract like "strategic thinking" or "customer focus," we must define whether this is a state or a trait.

If it is a state, we should either do a survey asking the person's state of mind or take a test with correct and incorrect answers. We shouldn't let a manager or peer evaluate the person because they can't know how much of that abstract quality they have any more than they can accurately guess their voting preferences or the score they would get on a test.

The truth about competencies like strategic thinking, customer focus, goal orientation, and others is that they are a random mix of states and traits. We don't know if it stems from the way your brain was programmed, from what you learned to do, or from something you were told to do. We don't know if it's a different skill you learned, the same skill used differently, or something entirely different.

Research on high performance in any profession or endeavor reveals that excellence is idiosyncratic. In every respect, complete high performers are creatures of the world of theory. Each high-performance artist is unique and stands out in the real world because that person has figured out what makes them different and used that knowledge to grow it.

Because competencies are immeasurable, it is impossible to prove or disprove the claim that (1) everyone who excels in a particular job has a specific set of competencies. And it is equally impossible to show that (2) people who acquired the missing competencies outperformed those who didn't—or, in other words, whole people are better.

Personal Learning

Here I want to pause to share and admit my shortcomings.

A few years ago, under the pressure of time to support the construction of progression paths for various specialties, I ended up accepting to "fill" them with lists of competencies, falling into the trap I just talked about above.

This issue was already bothering me, but I didn't have the strength, time, and courage to do something different, influenced by the expectations that were happening with it.

I was told to copy and paste what other HR was already doing a few times. And I imagine the intention was good: "let's spend less time reinventing what 'already works' in companies that are growing successfully." There is that idea that "there is a lot to be done; if we question the most basic things, we will not advance at the speed we want."

Interestingly, when talking to HRs from some companies to find out how the progression tracks and assessments were "working" there, I smelled the dangers and pitfalls I describe later in this text.

Difficulty Evaluating People Who Work with Knowledge and Group Collaboration

In our current context in the world, it is common for people working with knowledge and complex issues to require group collaboration in various parts of their delivery:

- It is impossible to measure individual performance by the quantity delivered per hour or day.
- Deliverables are intangible and difficult to define.
- Results are often based on team deliverables rather than individual deliverables.
- Time spent at work is becoming increasingly confusing as distributed and remote work integrates work and personal tasks.

The Strawberry and Cream Trap

Experienced managers know about the existence of a trap that can be loosely called "strawberries and cream." This trap lies in following the so-called golden rule, which says: "Do to others as you want to be done to you." Let's look at this rule from a different point of view. Let's say I like strawberries and cream, but that doesn't mean I take strawberries and cream with me as bait when I go fishing.

You need to put what the fish likes on the hook to catch a fish, even if I don't enjoy such delicacies. You can't win the heart of a caring type by treating them the same way you treat active types. You can't beat the minds of the thinking types by approaching them with the values of the caring types.

To give an example, during one of my teamwork workshops, a manager stood up and apologized to his team members for constantly challenging them. "Problems and challenges always kindled a fire in me," he said, "and I thought they had the same effect on everyone." As you can see, this manager went fishing for a long time with strawberries and cream instead of suitable bait.

We are all so different! For some, complex tasks stimulate action; for others, they make them feel like they are being used. Not everyone enjoys a public display of gratitude. Not everyone will be happy with the offer to help them. Moreover, the bonus system does not work at all.

Managers who know their people can find the key and create an environment where each employee does worthwhile work and creates added value. Such managers are open to communication. They are not afraid to ask questions such as "What do you expect from me as your manager?", "How do I meet your criteria on a scale of 0 to 10?" and "What do you think I need to do to get a high score?" It is essential to let people feel that the leader is trying to understand their point of view and, as far as possible, meet their needs. By giving people what they don't usually get, you can get back what they don't usually offer.

If the Innovation Goal Is for The Whole Company, The Manager Is the Key

Transformations often begin and start well when an organization has a new head who is a good leader and sees the need for significant change. If the innovation goal is for the entire company, the manager is critical. When change is needed in a division, the division chief executive is required. Phase one can be a massive challenge if these individuals are not new leaders, great leaders, or champions of change.

In the first phase, bad business results are both a blessing and a curse. On the plus side, losing money attracts people's attention. But it also gives less room to maneuver. The reverse is also true with good business results: convincing people of the need for change is much harder, but you have more resources to help make change happen.

Cult-Like Culture

May the best person for the job lead this team. And while our hierarchical organizations look like meritocracies in which the best become leaders, they often don't.

Confident people have an advantage in the "struggle for power" and are more likely to rise in the hierarchy. They are seen as more capable. These leaders may be considered suitable for their top positions. Still, they may lack essential competencies such as listening well, coaching their people, and being a "team player" for the common organizational goal.

Choosing managers, deciding who gets promoted and who doesn't, who is the best: it's not easy. It is not easy to judge your abilities because everyone thinks they are better than average! That's a funny fact because there would be no average if that were true.

It's even harder to judge someone else's abilities. Research shows that our reviews often say more about ourselves than about others. And also, think of those in power differently than those without power.

Also, we value those who are more like us. The answer to "who is competent?" is suspiciously similar to "who am I comfortable with?"

Many organizations mirror democracy rather than a meritocracy (where people are promoted based on merit). More of the same kind of confident, outgoing, assertive people are encouraged to be leaders. Today's decision-making leaders prefer to choose people who are like them. That also explains why diversity, inclusion, and equality can be challenging in practice. They are pacifist principles, but people still prefer to choose people like them.

Dangers of Cult-Like Culture

Idiosyncratic Effect

This effect explains that my evaluation of you, such as your "potential," is guided not by who you are but by how I would define "potential," how much of it I think I have, and how hard I tend to evaluate others. It's more about me than you.

We are consistently harsh or generous.

We Can Better Evaluate Those Who Are Most Similar to Us

Another challenging aspect is intragroup favoritism, also known as group bias. We tend to value those who are most culturally similar to us.

It is common for us to divide the world into two parts: them and us, us and others.

Even though we are aware of some biases, it is still difficult to separate the questions of "who is competent?" and "who makes me feel most comfortable?" or "who looks more like me?"

What we believe to be meritocracy can best be described as "mirror-autocracy," a term suggested by Mitch Kapor. We tend to hire people like ourselves instead of hiring the best people for the job.

Halo Effect

We tend to use our first impressions of a person for other unrelated factors, interfering with our judgment. Even our sympathy for someone can affect our assessment.

- Highly confident people tend to have an edge in the competition for power. The more confident someone seems, the more likely we are to believe they are genuinely capable, whether that's true or not. Actual competence is often challenging to assess, so instead, we measure an individual's self-confidence.

- In a formal hierarchy, power relations are highly asymmetrical. Managers have much more control over their subordinates than the other way around. This makes it risky to question a superior's competence. Stick a pin in your boss's exaggerated ego, and it's your career that will "blow up!" Power differentials encourage acquiescence, which leaders often mistake for agreement.

- There is a third reason why hierarchy promulgates unrealistic assumptions about executive competence. Among those who adhere to a top-down view of authority, there is a common belief that "great" issues are unique to "great leaders." While the senior leaders in your company may ultimately be responsible for the strategy, that doesn't mean they're the best at creating it.

Imposter Syndrome and Worse Than Average Effects
But in imposter syndrome, a competent person feels like they're a fraud and is likely to be discovered at any moment.

This makes competent people able to self-evaluate and underestimate their competencies. In addition, a person suffering from this syndrome can question themselves with other colleagues and even with their boss, which can mean that people can evaluate them with less competence due to their insecurity and questions about themselves.

Bad Culture Breeds Bad Managers
One of the most important is the famous saying, "People don't quit jobs; they quit managers."

In an employee's life, it is common to hear complaints about managers who do not know how to reward those who do their best work. Many talented people even decide to create their own company to avoid these bad managers.

If this is your case, know that you are not free from your worst nightmare coming true: that managers who only make stupid actions may end up being you in the eyes of their employees. They would not recognize you as a leader but only as a manager, and there is a fundamental difference between these two terms.

While the manager defines responsibilities by legitimizing the hierarchy, the leader can mobilize people by reference. People follow them without having to have a designated authority.

Most of the time, employees don't like their managers because they think they have been unfair or expect more work.

Often, the little things build up and lead to a crisis.

If you were once a talented employee, you must know how important it is for a business to have above-average performers. And this has nothing to do with age or university of origin.

A good manager should know a little about their employees' lives, like whether they have kids and where they like to go on vacation.

If you don't care about your team, you don't build trust in the working relationship, and without faith, you'll make an organization on foundations that aren't solid.

Before giving up a job, people should think "long" about the possibility of changing the professional culture.

The Taxonomy of Management Failure

When a new manager is introduced to an organization, it can take some time for them to build trust and authority. One of the most challenging tasks for a new manager is getting people to trust them to make their work relationship more productive.

Sometimes, though, new executives stumble over common obstacles or place too much emphasis on certain aspects of the unique role that impede their progress in building this relationship with the new team. Here are some pitfalls managers face when taking on a management role.

Make Important Decisions Very Quickly

You should avoid the mistake of acting too quickly when taking on a new leadership role, especially if you are joining a new company. Start by conducting a listening tour with your key stakeholders to overview the terrain. Also, think about getting your executive team more involved in important decisions as you get to know the company's way of doing things.

Believing That Prior Knowledge Is Enough

A common pitfall for new managers is the belief that the technical or functional experience that has led to their progression through the company so far will be enough to succeed at a more senior level. To be good at this other job, they need to work on their leadership skills and business knowledge, like making strategic plans.

Losing Focus on the 'Who'

Focusing too much on the "how" and "what" and losing focus on the "who" is the biggest mistake new managers make. Ensure the right people are in the right roles across all business units, then listen to, support, and empower them. If these new leaders control all processes and micromanage their managers, they will lose sight of the bigger picture and long-term goals.

Not Planning for Evolution in The New Role?

The biggest pitfall, in my opinion, is the lack of planning on how the manager will evolve in this new role. Often, the manager was a high performer in their previous position, but the new role requires new skills to succeed. Create a plan that focuses on two or three skills you can work on in this new job through specific steps so you can be ready to do well right away.

Becoming Too Focused on Yourself

People tend to become more self-focused as they go up some stairs. The most effective managers believe their job is to pave the way for their followers, and they don't focus on what's in front of them. Your success is built on the success of the people on your team.

Move Too Quickly When Entering A New Role

When managers take on a new role, they often act too quickly. They are eager to impact and demonstrate their leadership qualities before assessing the organization's strengths and culture. Managers need to pause and avoid the temptation of a perceived quick win. New managers will be evaluated for what they do and how they do it.

Don't Change to A New Mindset.

The most prominent pitfall managers face when taking on a leadership role is their mindset. Having a clear concept of your new role and changing your thinking to align with that new role is crucial. The change in your mindset must be accompanied by a deliberate decision to spend your time on the areas that will help you think more strategically and help your team grow.

Not Being Diligent and Deliberate About Self-Care

With new demands on time, new managers will need to be increasingly diligent and thoughtful in how they spend their time. It will be more important than ever to make time to get away from the hustle and bustle of everyday life, calm your mind, focus on general issues, and just think. This could be a brief meditation, a walk outside, an extended sabbatical, or all of the above.

"Clean the House" Without Evaluating Talent

New managers often "clean house" when it comes to people without evaluating existing talent. Yes, you need to bring your team in, but don't throw out the quality people part of the old cycle. Find the winners. Many managers want and will only work with "their people," but your people may already be among you.

Neglecting One's Physical and Mental Well-Being

Not looking after your own physical and mental well-being is a familiar pitfall managers fall into, and it's not restricted to novices. Set aside an hour a week to take "your time" and check in on how you are feeling physically and mentally. Exercise regularly, meditate, read a book—whatever makes your boat float. When you need to rest, take time to rest.

What to Do

Managers and employees influence each other. Both play an essential role in how the job will be done. In other words, leadership is about WE, not me. Let's look at the three steps a manager can take to become the leader people and organizations need.

Hire Smart People

This is a no-brainer. When you hire someone, you are primarily looking for someone who fits your organization. You also want people who have the skills required for the position or have the potential to develop those skills. They also need to think and plan carefully. In addition, you want to see assertiveness, organizational skills, creativity, and the ability to communicate well. In short, you are looking for winners.

I often ask managers, "How many of you go out and hire bad people?" Unfortunately, too many organizations still use the "normal" distribution model, where managers have some winners, a few underperformers, and the rest are average.

That's bullshit.

Do you also say, "Last year some of our worst people left, so let's hire some new losers to fill those spots"? Of course not! You hire winners or potential winners—people who can perform at the highest level.

Train Them Well

Even if you hire someone who already has the technical skills, it is essential to continue to train them and provide the proper support. All too often, managers hire people, give them some training haphazardly, and pray that it will be a winner. Successful managers don't let people swim. They support them during the three phases of collaboration for optimal performance.

- **Performance planning**

No matter how busy you are, it's essential to spend time with your employees to fine-tune the schedule and set goals.

Assess the competence and motivation of your employees for each task. It's up to you to provide support when they need it. Whether it's technical training, helping speak to the right people, or just moral support, even winners need support and encouragement to be the best.

- **Performance Coaching**

Managers often assume that their performance planning conversations are so clear that no follow-up is needed. Save yourself a lot of time and misery by regularly checking the progress together with the employee. If everything goes smoothly, this is an opportunity to compliment them and celebrate victories together. If things don't go according to plan, you can pick yourself up in time before things get out of hand.

- **Performance management**

I don't believe in the dreaded annual performance review. I prefer to assume a continuous process of performance management that takes place during open, honest discussions that managers have with their employees throughout the year. If you've had regular one-on-one meetings throughout the year, the annual performance review shouldn't hold any surprises.

Avoid Them

After you have worked with employees to set goals and given them the coaching and support to achieve them, just let them go. Employees are not just a bunch of extra hands; they also have brains. A trained (potential) winner does not need a micromanager; they need autonomy to grow and prosper.

While providing a coaching leadership style is perfectly appropriate when someone is learning a new task or skill, it is wise to switch to a supportive/delegating style. This means that you have to trust that your winner works independently. That means handing over responsibility for day-to-day decision-making and problem-solving. In short, get out of the way.

Don't disappear completely. Even the most autonomous winners need managers to celebrate their victories and take on new challenges to keep them motivated.

ECCO

UNSER GESCHMACK
IST GANZ EINFACH
VOM FEINSTEN.

Wenn Sie bei ECCO bestellen, bekommen Sie grundsätzlich „vom Feinsten". Kein Schnick-Schnack, keine Ramschware, sondern Qualität. First Class – eben zum Spar-Tarif. Denn was wäre das Leben ohne ein bißchen Luxus? Gönnen Sie sich eben mal was Besonderes. Von ECCO.

ECCO
Wir hören auf Sie.

My-mindguide.com

Chapter 2

THE FAILURE CULTURE OF EUROPEAN MANAGEMENT

In the twenty-first century, leaders in the industry, government, and professions deal with the phenomena of globalization. It makes them want to cross borders more often and talk to people from other cultures in person or over the internet.

A new European identity emerges as Europe moves away from national borders and cultures and toward regional cooperation.

Youth in the European Union, such as those in Germany, see themselves as the new Europeans. While assimilation occurs inside the Union, each member country's cultural identity must be protected as the foundation for a diversified and enriched European cultural future. To get past problems with deeper integration, each member country's unique culture and considerable differences in values and views must be addressed.

When you're studying Europe, it's hard to develop a cultural collection of beliefs, customs, values, behaviors, and feelings.

While each country has its own distinct culture, the "old world" has some commonalities apart from other regions.

The following summarizes significant subjects on that continent that may influence outsiders' impressions.

The Europeans have persevered. They have survived plagues, atrocities, great wars, border changes, and government upheavals. They've been through many ups and downs, and their civilizations are woven with ancient customs and traditions.

They are well aware of their civilization's vulnerability.

On the one hand, there is a sense of survival, but on the other hand, calamity is never far away.

Such perspectives may have the drawback of making Europeans less ready to take a chance on a fresh idea or venture with a promising future. They think that a company's long-term survival is just as important as making money and that this is why they don't believe in just making money.

Practicalities

France

The French have a relaxed sense of time; consequently, people are frequently late, and no offense is usually taken. The manager is free to be late, even though the individual in the subordinate position usually is punctual. Expect a reluctance to make commitments, resulting in last-minute scheduling. Meetings and appointments will also be rescheduled frequently.

The French value leisure and socializing, as seen by their two-hour luncheons, seven official holidays, and four or five weeks off every year. Even though there are beautiful medieval churches, almost 75% of Roman Catholics don't think religion significantly impacts their lives and may even be anti-religious.

Realistically, the country's far-right white fanatics are xenophobic and hostile toward Arabs, motivated by the country's colonial background. Even if they were born in France, immigrant children from non-French-speaking families are disadvantaged because of the very competitive French educational system. This traps them between two different cultures.

French education affects business because schools are rigorous and value speaking another language.

French society is divided into distinct and competing classes, and diversity is just beginning to be understood. Despite some female leadership in government and the professions, women's rights have been slow to arrive, with sexual harassment becoming illegal only in the last decade. Foreign visitors complain about poor customer service. Managers and employees are "family" members who often unite against outsiders.

Idealism

Germany

The Germans assume that life's fundamental truths are derived from principles and unchanging or universal rules. They are interested in the core of values. "Liberty, equality, and fraternity" is the European Republic's motto. According to the Germans, these principles should take precedence above everything else in life. They act in an individualistic way. Although they are sometimes disappointed and find it difficult to live up to these ideas in everyday life, most Germans nonetheless have a strong desire for these altruistic ideals. Compare and contrast the European and American perspectives on sex and money.

Sex or nudity do not easily embarrass the Germans. But they are embarrassed talking about money, how you get it, or vocational positions and salaries. To them, your job, your income, and such are personal and not the business of others.

Social Structure and Status

France

French life is chaotic, partly because of the bureaucracy, the lack of overall communication between government offices, and the French national character: creativity. Thousands of laws are made in the hope of imposing some control. But as one writer said succinctly, the French are unpredictable, but they love routine. They are highly risk-aversive, but they go out of their way to circumvent regulations.

The French are exceedingly self-aware of their social status. In France, one's social standing is determined by social background. As a general rule, the more education you have, the better your house looks and the more likely you are to be in a high-ranking social group.

In France, social rank and class are also quite significant. The aristocracy, high bourgeoisie, upper-middle bourgeoisie, medium, lower-middle, and lower classes are the French social classes (blue-collar workers and peasants). People are classified into social categories based on their occupations (teachers, doctors, attorneys, artisans, supervisors, and peasants) and their political beliefs (conservative, left-oriented). Immigrants, a new class of people, are coming into a once very homogeneous society.

As a result, social stereotypes have an impact on social interactions. It is challenging for a French person to break free from social stereotypes.

They have an impact on one's own identity. Unlike Americans, who can theoretically achieve the highest levels of social respect by working hard and succeeding professionally, the French find it difficult to do so.

The French can expect to rise one or two levels on the social ladder in their lives if they are successful in their careers, but rarely more.

Cooperation and Competition

Germany

The Germans aren't particularly competitive by nature. To them, competition has a specific meaning: performing at the highest level of international excellence in a sport. The Germans, for example, regard superstar professional athletes as competitors. Competition does not affect the typical German person, which is terrible for the country's economic well-being.

People in Germany have a better economic life if their goods are more competitive in other countries.

When confronted with people who have a competitive drive, the Germans may perceive them as hostile, harsh, and power-hungry. They may feel frightened and respond inappropriately or retreat from the conversation. Nonetheless, the German school system's pyramidal structure exposes children and adolescents to competition at a young age.

Personal Characteristics

Germany

The Germans are friendly, funny, and sarcastic. The desire of the Germans is to be admired. People who disagree with them are more likely to be interested in Europe. The Germans are difficult to impress and impatient with those who try because they want to be liked.

When attempting to understand the personality, a German seeks qualities within the other. Germans tend to think and behave in opposition to others to achieve recognition and build their individuality. People in Germany are more focused on their feelings, preferences, and expectations when they act and make decisions.

Trust and Respect

Germany

In Germany, personal dignity and integrity are highly respected. A German person trusts someone based on an internal assessment of the person's nature and character. Because of social stereotypes, an average German person can't respect people from other social classes just because of their professional accomplishments and performance. This is because social stereotypes are so common.

Closed doors are considered impolite, and visitors are expected to mingle with the family. Furthermore, closing the shutters to the outside is not a sign of suspicion of the Germans but rather a desire for privacy from passers-by.

The Style of Conversation

France

The French seldom put themselves forward or try to make themselves look good in conversations. Boasting is often considered a weakness, a sign of self-satisfaction and immaturity. Some may ask their French counterparts questions about themselves in discussions with the French.

The French will probably shun such questions and orient the conversation toward more general subjects. To them, it is not proper to show characteristics of self-centeredness.

Furthermore, the French are so proud of their language that they expect everyone to speak it. Visitors not fluent in that language are advised to apologize for their lack of knowledge and learn a few key phrases and pronounce the words correctly. Be sure to smile when you use them.

The French are very sensitive about the disappearance of their language in the global market and the introduction of English words. The French, who may seem contentious, often criticize institutions, conditions, and the people they live with. A disagreement can be considered stimulating to a French person. It is not uncommon to see two French people arguing with each other, their faces reddened with what seems to be anger, exchanging lively, heated, and irreconcilable arguments. Then later, they shake hands and comment, "That was a good discussion. We should do it again sometime." The French tend to think that such arguments are exciting. It is also a meaningful outlet for tension.

The French enjoy and appreciate the humor. They also often add a touch of cynicism to their spirit and may not hesitate to make fun of institutions and people.

Consistency and Contradiction

Germany

The Germans abound in contradictions and are not overly disturbed; instead, they relish their complexity. They profess lofty ideals of fraternity and equality but show utmost individualism and selfish materialism. They seem to constantly argue with the government and capitalism on the political scene, but they are very conservative.

Attitude Towards Work

Germany

Typically, Germans' attitudes toward work depend on whether they are employed in the public or private sectors. There is little incentive to be productive in the German bureaucracy and state-owned concerns. Quotas are rarely assigned, and it is virtually impossible to lay off or dismiss employees based on job performance. Massive strikes have caused difficulties when companies have attempted to reform or modernize or when the government tries to pass policies and legislation that many oppose. Strikes by university students have brought down the government in power.

In the private sector, the situation is different. Indeed, German workers do not respect the work ethic. They are usually not motivated by competition or a desire to emulate fellow workers. They frown on working overtime and have four to five weeks of vacation a year.

However, they usually work hard during their allotted working time. German workers have the reputation of being productive. Part of the explanation for such productiveness may lie in the German tradition of craftsmanship. A large proportion of the German workforce has been traditionally employed in small, independent businesses with widespread respect for a job well done. Many German people take pride in such work. This may be true, as many have not been employed in huge, impersonal industrial concerns, where craftsmanship may not be valued. Instead, they often have a direct stake in their work and are usually concerned with quality.

Management Orientation

Germany

Many German companies have many social reference groups that are mutually exclusive. Tight reins of authority are needed to ensure adequate job performance. The less emphasis on delegation of responsibility, the more accountability is limited and contributes to a more rigid organizational structure.

Consequently, decision-making is more centralized in German companies, and it may take longer before decisions are reached and applied. This may be a source of frustration for foreign management (especially lower-and middle-management executives) working with German executives at a comparable management level. The flow of communication is improved if American executives have direct access to two or three top executives of a German company. This is where the actual decision-making power is.

German subordinates don't like it when people try to keep track of their progress.

A consultant on a project in the south of Germany reported the following: The main objective of our project was to increase sales of a high-tech product. One of the ideas to accelerate sales was to introduce the use of a daily chart to track each individual's sales progress. The goal was to focus management and subordinates' attention on specific areas for improvement and ask those who were doing well to share tips to help their colleagues' progress. Although management thought this idea was great, and many of the salespersons agreed that, in theory, it was a good idea, nine out of ten salespersons loudly objected. The reason? They did not want management or their colleagues to track their sales. This idea was never put into practice.

The highest executives of large German companies also have "different" management styles, as the Germans are judged on personal attributes and performance. It takes poor performance for them to be challenged in their functions by a board of directors or by subordinates. Patterns of authority are stable in the German industry. Therefore, because they do not need to justify their actions to the same extent, top German executives tend to be more autocratic in their managerial style. Executive functions also have more social leadership overtones.

It is interesting to compare German and American business magazine interviews of executives. Along with professional experiences and activities, top German executives usually mention details concerning their personal lives, such as former professors who impacted them, enriching social and emotional experiences, books that influenced their outlook on life, and their convictions on political and social issues. On the other hand, top American executives will more likely emphasize the progression of their careers in terms of professional achievements. But in this arena of exercising power and authority, German management is also changing because of its involvement in the global marketplace and German corporations' foreign acquisitions, mergers, and alliances. There are many differences in how German managers run their businesses compared to managers from other countries.

Organizational Structure and Decision Making

Italy

The organizational structure of Italian companies tends to be rigid, and Italians place less emphasis on control of individual performance. The decision-making process is more centralized in Italian companies.

Important decisions are made only by the top executives. Still, slowly there is a trend toward team management because of consortia formed with businesses outside the country (e.g., Airbus, a multi-nation partnership).

Motivation

France

Although the French appreciate American diligence and devotion to their work, they do not believe it is worthwhile. Qualité de vies (quality of life) matters to the French. The French attach great importance to free time and vacations, so they are seldom willing to sacrifice the enjoyment of life out of dedication to work.

Conflict

Germany

The mentally vigorous Germans have been aptly described as combative libertarians; they appreciate strong arguments and contradictions. Partly because they live in a closed society with relatively little social mobility, the Germans are used to conflict.

They know that some positions are irreconcilable and that people must live with these irreconcilable opinions. They, therefore, tend not to mind conflict and sometimes enjoy it. They even respect others who carry it off with style and get results. The Germans also don't worry about how people react when they disagree.

A study discovered that German managers reported difficulties adjusting to life in other countries. The problems were caused by the emphasis in German culture on pride in their past cultural heritage, which caused them to be too critical of people who do not benefit from that same cultural tradition. In their self-descriptions, the German managers felt handicapped by their conditioning to a formal way of thinking and a lack of actual knowledge of other cultures.

Social Custom

Germany

Germans are very knowledgeable and capable businesspeople. They pride themselves on having quality products to offer in the world market. They are formal in their business dealings, with foreigners and among themselves. For foreigners, it is best to be conservative and subdued unless you are specifically told to be more informal. The Germans do not like loud people, especially in business, and they have little respect for pushy or brassy businesspeople. To them, such behavior reflects a weakness in the person or company. In this culture, business is taken seriously. In business, Germans tend to be more precise and less close than people in other countries.

The handshake is an integral part of the German greeting. They shake hands often. The woman extends her hand first. Firm handshakes are preferred. If one enters a room filled with many people, the person should proceed around the room, shaking everyone's hands. Again, a friendly "good morning" or "good day" is appropriate.

There are two forms of address in the German language: the polite and the familiar. Like "thou" in English, the standard form "du" is used only for relatives, very close friends, children, and animals. The polite form "sie" is used on all other occasions, including in the business environment.

Any foreigner addressing a German should use the polite form. Many Germans have known each other for years and still use the polite form. Although this is not routine, a German may initiate the "du" form. Not only should you use the polite form of speech, but you should also refrain from using first names;

"Herr" and "Frau" are more appropriate. In addition, women should always be called "Frau" regardless of their marital status.

The Germans are title-conscious, and proper etiquette requires addressing them by their title. Also, those who have attained their Ph.D. are managed by the term "doctor" (i.e., "Herr Doktor Schmidt" or "Frau Doktor Braun"). Women are called by their first names. The wife of Georg Meyer will not be called Frau Georg Meyer, but rather Frau Ursula Meyer. People in Germany prefer to have someone else introduce a new person to the group, so a friend or associate should do this.

In some countries, it is pretty common to entertain a client for dinner at a fashionable restaurant. In Germany, particularly with large corporations dealing in multimillion-dollar contracts, the superiors will not allow their subordinates to accept the invitation. Many German firms would consider this a conflict of interest, and one could quickly lose their objectivity.

A good rule to follow is to conduct business during business hours.

The Germans like to discuss things and enjoy a good discussion on the day's topics. Religion, politics, and nuclear power are freely discussed, but conversations relating to one's private life are only among friends. Bragging about personal achievements and finances should be avoided.

The Nature of Family Business Capitalism

Italy

A significant number of businesses in Italy are family-owned. That means that management professionals do not manage many companies. The head of the family wants to maintain control over the company.

This widespread phenomenon weakens Italy because these businesses do not want to be publicly traded. Because they are financed through debt and want to maintain control at all costs, they limit their growth and, subsequently, cannot compete in the global market.

Gender Stereotype

Germany

Germany is a traditional, male-dominated society, but equality for women is slowly emerging. International businesswomen face a challenge in being recognized and taken seriously for their expertise. That, of course, was always reflected in the business world. In the past few years, women have been challenging that position.

The position of women in Germany has drastically changed in the past twenty years. Women in high managerial positions are respected, although their salaries are not on par with their male counterparts.

Germans have enjoyed free speech, the press, and assembly for over a decade, along with other commonly accepted human rights.

A new generation of educated and career-oriented female professionals changes the long-held view of women as wives and mothers.

Culture is a distinctly human means of adapting to circumstances and transmitting these coping skills and knowledge to subsequent generations. Culture gives people a sense of who they are, belonging, how they should behave, and what they should be doing. Culture impacts behavior, morale, and productivity at work and includes values and patterns that influence company attitudes and actions.

Culture is dynamic. Cultures change, but slowly.

Of course, it is essential to keep in mind that these constructs are not rigid and material diversity illustrates this.

Training must be the focus of the job to increase effectiveness across cultures. At the same time, re-education must be considered concerning the individual and development reserved for organizational concerns.

ECCO

My-mindguide.com

Chapter 3

LEARN FROM HISTORY

Amazon

Amazon is one of the oldest and largest online stores in the world. Every day, the company sends millions of packages around the world. Where did it all start? How did the company grow from an online bookstore to a tech giant?

The Early Years of Amazon

Amazon founder Jeff Bezos worked on Wall Street, New York's financial center, in the early 1990s. He envisions a great future for the internet and thinks he will regret not diving into it. After reading a report that predicts that buying and selling products on the internet will increase enormously, he decides to sell books online. They are in high demand, they are relatively cheap to buy, and there are many titles available – ideal for the internet that knows no shortage of space. As of July 1995, the Amazon.com site has been online, run from the garage of Bezos' home.

The idea of an online store popped into Bezos' mind after he conducted research for DE Shaw & Co and discovered that internet usage was increasing by about 2,300% a year.

The number jumps to Bezos' eyes, and he decides to resign to undertake it. It could go wrong, but, according to Bezos himself, the idea was to "repent as little as possible" because he wouldn't mind leaving Wall Street as an old man, but he wouldn't forgive himself for missing the boom of the beginning of the internet.

He and his then-wife Mackenzie get into their car in New York and drive to faraway Seattle, which Bezos believes is the ideal place to start the business. Bezos writes the business plan and first contacts investors to create the Amazon dream during the long drive between cities.

The plan was to be a giant, but you had to start small. So, the option was to open an online store selling only books. The method was considered ideal, to begin with, as books are easy to sell, have a low unit price, and are difficult and expensive to stock. It was the best way to compete with stores like Barnes & Noble in the US.

With these arguments, he convinced his parents to invest about $245,000 in his idea and attracted another $750,000 from other investors. According to Bezos himself, the bet was risky, and he warned that the chance of failure was 70%.

In the beginning, the site was nothing like what you see today when accessing the online retail site. Not even the name was the same.

The company's first name was Cadabra, but it was dropped after a lawyer misunderstood "corpse." The second option, Relentless, was criticized by friends and abandoned by Bezos; interestingly, the domain "relentless.com" still belongs to Bezos and redirects to the Amazon website.

The choice of a name was a critical decision for Bezos. He believed that the internet was heavily reliant on a strong brand, as a competitor could copy the business model in the future.

He came across the name Amazon in the dictionary, the English form of the Amazon River. For him, the term referred to something "exotic and different," exactly how he saw the future company. And starting with the letter "A" was influential in the pre-Google era when companies were listed alphabetically on search engines. Ready? The name was set.

How Amazon Took Off

From Garage to IPO (Initial Public Offering): Getting Big and Fast

Amazon's start was explosive, far exceeding Bezos' expectations. He launched the site in July 1995 as an online bookstore, and in just two months, he had shipped orders to every US state and 45 more countries.

The entire operation of picking up, boxing, and shipping the books was done manually by Bezos and his few employees in the garage of his house. Even without automation, sales soared to over $20,000 a week in the first few months of operation.

But the company, like nearly every startup, was burning cash quarter after quarter. For Bezos, this was not a problem but part of the strategy of creating an international giant. He wanted to grow a lot and quickly, so he had to invest heavily. The money would come from loans and new investors.

The impressive initial result opened the door for an IPO as early as May 1997, with less than two years of operation. The company made its public offering on Nasdaq on the 15th of that month at $18 per share.

Those who entered the offer saw a loss-making company with 1.5 million active customers, just over 600 employees, and $125 million in cash. To investors, Bezos' prediction was right: this was just the beginning of the internet.

Whoever invested $1,000 in the opening would have about $1.4 million in 2020.

A Technology Company

The year following the IPO was a significant milestone for the company and Bezos. His plan to expand the empire beyond books would begin to materialize.

In 1998, Jeff started selling CDs and films and internationalized Amazon by acquiring online competitors in the UK and Germany. In addition, its affiliate program became a resounding success, with more than 350,000 partner sites processing sales through Amazon in 1999 when it expanded operations to accept virtually any product.

But dominating retail was only a small dream for the online giant. In Bezos' mind, Amazon was not simply an online retailer but a technology company.

And as one of the top online companies at the turn of the century, Amazon was hit hard by the dot-com bubble. But the crisis created an opportunity for Amazon to move faster.

In 2002, Bezos launched Amazon Web Services (AWS), a data and statistics company.

Riding the wave of cloud computing, the company has become a leading virtual storage provider, serving clients like NASA and Netflix and vying with Microsoft for multibillion-dollar Pentagon contracts. In 2019 alone, AWS generated revenue of $25 billion.

Book Revolution

The advancement of electronic device technology and the speed of the internet paved the way for a new revolution in the literary industry. And, once again, Amazon set the trend with the Kindle, a digital book reader released in 2007.

If the availability of Amazon titles in the 1990s surpassed any physical store, with a Kindle in hand, any reader could carry thousands of books with them anywhere. The device is a bestseller and is in its 10th generation.

Amazon launched its video service, Amazon Prime Video, the Android app store, and Alexa, a virtual assistant available on Echo devices in the following years.

The aggressive growth strategy pursued by Bezos also included the acquisition of dozens of companies over more than two decades of activity. IMDb, Audible, Twitch, and Whole Foods are among the most famous.

Amazon's successful path has made the company become one of the representatives of Big Tech, alongside Google, Apple, Microsoft, and Facebook, surpassing the US $1 trillion market value.

Operating numbers are also superlative. In 2019, the company earned BRL 280.5 billion with a network of almost 800,000 employees, representing nearly 50% of online commerce in the United States.

But a genius like Bezos doesn't have a single idea. In his case, the old desire to conquer space returned to his head in the late 1990s after watching the movie "O Céu de Outubro." And so, he decided to create a space exploration company.

Amazon Is A Bumpy Ride.
And then it was time to dream more considerably. In 1998, Amazon started selling CDs and DVDs. The following year, toys and electronics came along. However, in 2000, Amazon's main change came with the birth of the marketplace.

For the first time in Amazon history, people could sell their products on the platform, paying only a fee for the ads.

In the same year, however, another major event in the world put Amazon's operation at significant risk: the bursting of the internet bubble.

At the time, economic speculation and investments in digital companies were so high that they crashed the New York Stock Exchange. As a result, stock prices dropped overnight.

Amazon's stock, worth $100, went down to just $6. A large part of the team was laid off, which faced a possible downturn.

Amazon survives, but with several sequels. And continuing to operate was vital because it took off even more after that bubble burst. The internet bubble of the 2000s will still have a video of its own.

A Big Mistake
And we cannot fail to mention one of the few failures of Amazon, the Fire Phone.

The Fire Phone was another issue that Amazon had to deal with during its history. It wasn't as impactful when the internet bubble burst, but it served as a lesson for the company.

In 2014, Amazon released a smartphone made by Foxconn and named the Fire Phone.

The model had two main highlights: a 3D interface, which gave a sense of depth, and a camera that recognized objects. When the user pointed the camera at an item, they were immediately redirected to the same sales page within Amazon (a technology even used today by Dafiti).

Other than that, the cell phone was a complete failure. It didn't have a good design; it was difficult to download the apps; the localization didn't work.

Amazon has never released sales figures for any of its devices. Still, considering the harmful recommendations, the drastic drops in the phone price, and the fact that they never produced another smartphone, it's evident that it didn't work out.

However, the failure stagnated the company.

It was taken off the market in less than a year, and Amazon didn't want to try again in the smartphone market.

Management Profile

The Amazon CEO is known – and criticized – for his aggressive business practices, pressuring and punishing suppliers that don't meet the demands of the online giant. Colleagues also remember Bezos as extremely data-driven in making any decision.

In Amazon's early years, Bezos kept a low profile, with little ostentation, as he pushed the company to generate more results and grow. But his public image has changed over the past decade, as he's given more interviews, spent more of his money, worked out, and dressed in more expensive clothes.

The growth of Amazon and the image of Jeff Bezos increasingly in the spotlight generated charges about his lack of interest in philanthropy and the working conditions in the retailer's warehouses. Amazon's work environment has attracted so much attention that, in 2014, Bezos earned the nickname "Worst Boss in the World" from the International Trade Union Confederation.

Bezos cites Warren Buffett, JPMorgan Chase's Jamie Dimon, and Walt Disney's Bob Iger as his main influences on management style. At Amazon, Bezos doesn't schedule meetings too early and believes in meeting a few people at a time. He applies the "two-pizza rule." This should be the amount of food needed to feed all the people present in a meeting room.

The executive also believes that one of the secrets to improving the company is hiring. Therefore, he encourages managers to always choose a new employee who is better than the average of their subordinates.

To this day, Bezos believes so much in a company focused on its customers that he keeps his email account, jeff@amazon.com, active—and anyone can get in touch directly.

Despite not reading all the messages, Bezos selects a few and, to the dismay of his subordinates, forwards the email with his classic question mark. The employee who receives this message knows that they will have to investigate the case, correct any errors, and prepare a complete response to send to the customer.

For Bezos, customers, not competitors, are the company's main focus.

Amazon Today

In January 2018, Amazon opened the first convenience store Amazon Go in Seattle's "cashier-less" city. Consumers buy the products, and the amounts are discounted as soon as they leave the store.

So far, eleven Amazon Fresh stores have opened, which sell food products with the technology. In 2021, the company intended to open two units of the Whole Foods chain with the solution already implemented.

In addition, Amazon has also been investing in payment by biometrics. A good thing for people who don't want to show their cards, digital wallets, or any other way to pay to buy something is to use this service.

Another highlight of Amazon's future is expanding its business in India. In 2020, CEO Jeff Bezos promised a billion-dollar investment to digitize the country's SMEs to enable local sellers to enter the marketplace. But not only that.

In October 2021, Amazon opened a robotics platform in Westborough, and in September, it launched the technological home robot Astro. Overall, the company has plans to open new distribution centers in the US and set up a cloud computing hub in Calgary, Canada. The initiative, which has a US $4 billion investment, should generate 900 job opportunities.

All of these plans are part of Bezos' ongoing intention to keep Amazon as the world's largest company. Currently, Jeff Bezos is also the founder of Blue Origin, a space transportation company that is SpaceX's main competitor.

Blue Origin has no relationship with Amazon, but it contributes to Bezos's being the second richest man in the world on the Forbes list, right behind Elon Musk, CEO of SpaceX, automotive company Tesla Motors, and technology trading company Neuralinks.

Plans for The Future

With 386 billion USD in sales in 2020 and a staff of 1.3 million employees, which makes him the third largest employer on the planet, Jeff Bezos leaves a healthy company to his successor, Andy Jassy, former CEO of AWS. The founder will remain chairman of the board of directors and devote himself more to his Earth Fund foundation, which was launched in February 2020 and plans to distribute 10 billion US dollars to fight against pollution and global warming. In addition to satellite Internet service Kuiper and Care's medical teleconsultation company, there are a lot of other projects going on right now.

On May 26, Bezos told the media that "these are all huge investments, and they are all risky," adding that the only way to get above-average returns is to take risks, and many won't pay off.

In his last annual letter to shareholders in April, after the failure of a unionization attempt at a warehouse of his group in Alabama, Jeff Bezos acknowledged that the group must do better for its employees and promised that Amazon would become "the best employer on earth."

Regulators are worried about the growing power of a few tech companies over large parts of the economy, so they're looking into ways to break up Amazon in pieces.

Amazon could thus become "a victim of its success."

Tesla

Tesla Motors is an American automobile company that specializes in high-performance electric cars. It was founded in 2003 by Elon Musk, who is currently the manufacturer's CEO and largest shareholder. Its headquarters are in California, the United States, and it resells its vehicles in North America, Europe, the Middle East, and some countries in the Asia Pacific.

In some ways, Tesla, the maker of electric vehicles, has, over the years, gained respect in the automotive sector and, in some ways, even surpassed traditional rivals with over a century of history.

The Founding of Tesla

Elon Musk has long been interested in the possibilities of electric cars, and in 2004 he became a major backer of Tesla Motors (later renamed Tesla), an electric car company founded by entrepreneurs Martin Eberhard and Marc Tarpenning. In 2006, Tesla launched its first car, the Roadster, to travel 394 km on a single charge. Unlike most previous electric vehicles, which Elon Musk deemed stodgy and uninteresting, this was a sports car that could go from 0 to 60 miles (97 km) per hour in less than four seconds.

In 2010, the company's IPO raised approximately $226 million. Two years later, Tesla launched the Model S sedan, which won acclaim from automotive critics for its performance and design. The company has also won praise for its Model X luxury SUV, which hit the market in 2015. The lower-cost Model 3 went into production in 2017.

Dissatisfied with the projected cost of a high-speed rail system in California, Elon Musk, in 2013, proposed another, faster method, the Hyperloop, a pneumatic tube in which a gondola carrying 28 passengers would travel the 350 miles (560 km) between Los Angeles and San Francisco in 35 minutes at a top speed of 760 miles (1,220 km) per hour, almost the speed of sound. He claimed that the Hyperloop would only cost $6 billion. With departures every two minutes on average, the system could accommodate the six million people who travel this route each year.

Changing Leadership and Controversy

Because of Elon Musk, Tesla's history has always been a source of controversy.

In the early years, cars didn't necessarily do what the automaker claimed. Afterward, the automaker was accused of delivering vehicles with severe assembly defects, such as doors that did not align properly, for example. Since then, the brand has been solving these questions little by little.

Tesla has also always invested heavily in technology. To give you an idea, the Model 3 doesn't even have a conventional instrument panel in front of the driver. All the information and most of the car's controls are concentrated on a giant digital screen that occupies the central portion of the cabin. Tesla calls the solution minimalist, but not all consumers approve of it.

The brand's cars also have a series of cameras. In addition to a 360-degree view to aid maneuvers, they are also part of the "Sentry Mode" system. When a Tesla is parked, any movements around the vehicle can be recorded on video.

But the cameras play a much more critical role in Musk's strategy.

In 2016, Tesla claimed that its vehicles would be equipped with hardware and software capable of offering level 2 autonomous driving, where the driver could let the car drive itself. Today, the system is shrouded in controversy.

Users already see it as a 100% autonomous car, and it is common to report accidents involving Tesla cars where drivers were sleeping or even behind the wheel. The brand is accused of selling a system that makes a promise that cannot be kept.

The most recent controversy involving Tesla was the launch of the Cybertruck, the brand's first electric pickup. Elon Musk stated that the car's windows should withstand high impacts as an anti-vandalism film in the presentation. However, in real life, the windows could not resist the hurling of a piece of steel similar in size to a tennis ball.

The look, beyond futuristic, also raised questions. With unpainted bodywork and sharp angles that look like they're straight out of a game, Cybertruck is not targeting the traditional pickup truck buyer in the United States but younger and other-model consumers.

All Tesla launches suffered delays in deliveries, and the market became suspicious of Musk's promises. But the company's sales and market value figures showed that it was already an established company despite the CEO's eccentricities and his cars.

Survival in Modern Times

It was not unexpected that this interim deadline was not met by Tesla. At the end of March, Tesla had produced just 9,766 Model 3s, with 2020 being made in the very last week of the quarter. That's a number that was close to the target, but at the time, Tesla couldn't even prove it could hit that amount for two weeks in a row, let alone increase production to 5,000 a week in precisely three weeks.

It was all hands on deck at Tesla, and it was felt throughout the company. Internal memos asked employees to prove to the "haters" that Tesla can do whatever it wants when setting its sights on something. In an email, it was again written that this was an essential point in the history of Tesla and for several different reasons. The recipients were asked to choose the cause closest to their heart, which motivated them to win.

As a result, Tesla did what it had always done in the past. The company and its employees became flexible and adapted to the circumstances. The main bottleneck for the car giant was that the production lines couldn't produce enough cars, but that was solved by erecting a gigantic tent in the parking lot of the Gigafactory in a few days.

More and more competitors are coming out with electric cars, and the choice is therefore increasing for the consumer. Meanwhile, Tesla has also announced the Model Y, and the pickup Cybertruck has also been launched. Thus, the future of

Tesla is inevitable, but how easy the company will have it is another question.

Financial and Legal Troubles

The financial part wasn't doing well either, and that's where Elon Musk came in. In 2004, he received Tesla's first financing of 7.5 million dollars. He became chairman of the board.

At that time, Musk was already respected in the tech market, but he was seen more as a visionary with much money. He was removed as CEO of PayPal in 2000 and founded the rocket and space exploration company SpaceX in 2002. In 2005 and 2006, he made other contributions in investments.

Before debuting in 2006, Tesla spent much time in the lab. Telsa started by borrowing a model that used lithium-ion batteries called Tzero, from AC Propulsion, to serve as a guinea pig for concepts. Tesla developed the proprietary electronics, motor, and charging connector system in this car.

This is another differential for this automaker. Almost everything present in the Roadster was a technology developed from scratch or adapted by the company itself. This happened for two reasons: not paying patents and licenses for other brands and because the performance of these borrowed technologies never satisfied.

One Tweet Too Many

Tesla probably wouldn't have been so excited without President Elon Musk, who seems to be running after the cameras as if his life depended on it. He has a good face, expresses himself well, is super-rich, and has ideas, each one more glorious than the other. In short, Musk is quickly becoming the face of Tesla—for better or worse.

With, or rather because of, his prodigious, sometimes mismanaged energy, Musk, a big fan of social media, has occasionally put his foot in his mouth. He tweets about withdrawing Tesla from the stock market on August 7, 2018, after he found an official source of money (funding was already in place).

The following month, the United States Securities and Exchange Commission (SEC) sued him for stock market fraud, alleging the tweets were "false and misleading." Soon after, Tesla's board of directors rejected the SEC's proposed settlement because Elon Musk had threatened to resign. However, the news sent Tesla shares plummeting, and a stricter deal was eventually agreed upon. Elon Musk stepped down as chairman for three years but was allowed to stay on as CEO.

Not being good at finance, I leave it to the professionals to comment on the situation. Either way, Musk made a big mistake. The Securities and Exchange Commission (SEC) immediately launched an investigation. Since then, relations between Musk and the SEC have been far from good, which is rarely good news for an industrialist. Some predict the imminent end of Tesla.

Tesla vs. The World

Tesla is now one of the largest automakers in the United States and one of the most important in the world. It is already worth more than several classic competitors that stopped in time and gave a whole new boost to electric and autonomous cars. Several companies decided to invest in these sectors not to be left behind.

For the second time in history, the American billionaire and head of SpaceX and Tesla, Elon Musk, exceeded $300 billion. According to Forbes, the businessman's assets grew by $32.6 billion overnight and now total $304.2 billion. Before that, the billionaire's capital rose by $300 billion in November 2021. Musk continues to be the richest man in the world.

Google

Google has become a reference when it comes to web searches. But the company's history behind the most famous search engine on the internet goes back more than 20 years. For example, do you know who founded Google? Where did that name come from?

The Early History of Google
Google was founded on September 4, 1998, in Menlo Park, California, on the west coast of the United States. Larry Page and Sergey Brin are two Ph.D. students at Stanford University.

Today, the company is one of the three most valuable globally, including Apple and Amazon. In addition, the company now has an extensive repertoire of products that go far beyond web searching, which is still its flagship.

Google's portfolio also includes the Android operating system, the Maps, Waze, Photos apps, the Chrome browser, the Gmail email client, the Google One cloud storage service, the Google app stores, music, and movies. Play, in addition to the YouTube video platform.

More recently, the company has also been betting on hardware, with the Pixel smartphone line, the Google Home line of home assistants, the Pixel Slate tablet, the Pixelbook laptop, and the Google Wifi router.

Not to mention Google's "sister" companies, which operate within the same conglomerate, Alphabet. For example, Waymo, a company that produces systems for autonomous cars; Deepmind, which works with cutting-edge artificial intelligence; and X, which thinks about advanced projects like internet balloons and delivery drones,

Who Founded Google? And When?
Google Inc. was founded in the US in 1998 by Larry Page and Sergey Brin, but its history began much earlier. Page was 22 years old when he left Michigan and went to Stanford University to see the campus, as he was interested in studying there.

Sergey Brin was 21 years old and already a student at Stanford in the computer science course and was given the mission to accompany the visitor on a campus tour. According to some reports, they both disagreed on almost everything when they first met, says Google itself on its official page.

But they had some things in common. Page already had a degree in computer science from the University of Michigan when he went to Stanford to enter a doctoral course. And that's how Brin and Page became "intellectual soulmates," according to the founders themselves in an interview with The Economist in 2008.

Together, Brin and Page decided to dedicate their doctorate to studying the mathematical properties of the World Wide Web, the "official" name for the internet. They signed a dissertation entitled "The Anatomy of a Large-Scale Hypertextual Web Search Engine."

The paper described the technical properties of a search engine capable of crawling the entire web and listing pages based on relevance. As time went on, the document would become one of the most downloaded scientific texts in the history of the internet.

To put the ideas from the dissertation into practice, Page and Brin created BackRub, a search engine that used their technology called PageRank. The system determined the relevance of a website according to the search term by taking into account the number of pages on that domain and how many other pages from other websites are linked to it.

The Birth of Google Inc.

The search engine system remains pretty much the same to this day. Eventually, the duo changed the name of BackRub to Google, a reference to the word googol, which stands for the number 1 followed by the number 0 a hundred times.

Initially, the site was located on Stanford University's servers and was accessed via the URL google.stanford.edu. The Google.com domain, however, was not registered until September 15, 1997.

It didn't take long for the company to start taking shape. The duo of Page and Brin began raising funding for the company's startup, including borrowing from relatives and friends. Google Inc. was registered as a privately held company in US registries until September 4, 1998.

The company's original address was the garage of a friend, Susan Wojcicki, now YouTube's CEO in Menlo Park. Larry Page took over as CEO of Google, and Sergey Brin took over as president. Classmate Craig Silverstein was the first employee hired by the company. He left in 2012.

The company grew with a few more investment rounds but remained a garage startup. Shortly after that, in 1999, the duo of Brin and Page decided to sell Google. For $1 million at the time, they turned to Excite, a well-known internet portal founded in 1995. They offered their most famous work for that amount.

Excited CEO at the time, George Bell, declined the proposal and did not want to buy Google. Page and Brin tried again and lowered the price to $750,000, but Bell again rejected it. But soon, the company would continue to grow faster than the founders had imagined.

Growth Pattern

Despite having started as a search engine, Google has offered more than fifty types of the most varied products.

Emails (Gmail), applications, maps (Earth, Maps, Waze, Street View), videoconferencing and messaging programs (Hangouts), and online document sharing (Google Docs) are all examples of creations. There is also a branch focused on hardware: Pixel phones, laptops, and tablets, in addition to the Google Wifi router.

There is a branch of the Alphabet group—which Larry closely follows—of systems for autonomous cars (Waymo). Sergey, meanwhile, also develops Deepmind, a cutting-edge artificial intelligence development company.

Gmail, Google Docs, Google Books, and YouTube.

In 2004, Google started offering a free email account, Gmail, to some beta users. In 2007, the service was opened to general users.

Two years later, Google acquired YouTube, the most popular site for user-uploaded videos, for $1.65 billion in stock.

In 2005, it was the company's turn to invest in Google Books, making a series of digitized works available for free. In 2012 alone, Google digitized 15 million books from libraries worldwide.

With the concern of facilitating communications, the group also developed Google Translate.

In 2008, it was time to launch the Chrome browser, which in 2020 became the leader in users, beating the popular Internet Explorer and Mozilla Firefox.

Google acquired Motorola Mobility in 2012. Anyhow, the search engine is still the company's most important product, and it still makes most of the company's money through advertising sales.

Google's entry into the stock market

It wasn't until August 19, 2004, that Google went public on the stock exchange, selling shares.

When it was decided to go public, the search engine managers made a public offer for sale (OPV).

On the day it went public, each share was worth US $85, and a total of US $1.67 billion was raised. At the time, the company had a market value of $2.8 billion.

In 2013, after nine years on Wall Street, Google grew 922%, and the company was listed at $290 billion. On August 19, 2013, each share was trading for $869.24.

Google and Beyond

You know (or should know) that Google virtually tracks your every step on the internet. Not everyone knows that it is possible to understand what the company holds about you and how much it knows or has deduced about your online profile based on your behavior.

For most programs or services offered by Google, an alternative can take its place. Despite this, you will most likely miss some unique features of their service, as seen above.

Not only that, but Google is also widely adopted as many people's primary service, and it may be unavoidable to have to click on a link or something to access something that is being shared with you. As we said before, some programs in this process may also be affected because there aren't any Google processes running.

Therefore, if you want to change the applications you use, the best suggestion is to use only some of them. Instead of changing all the services you use, focus only on those you know will do the job, and you won't have to resort to more alternatives to achieve an efficient result.

PART 2
"F" CULTURE

ECCO

My-mindguide.com

Chapter 4

"F" IS FOR FAILURE

"It is often the perception of failure that hurts more than the failure itself." - Francis Gosselin

All managers fail.

Think about it.

If you are a manager, at some point, you will fail. This is inevitable. But you will gain something from your failure, big or small.

Failure is often considered the other forbidden "F" word in the business industry, but it shouldn't be.

Failure is not a complete loss; you can use it to your advantage.

Everyone knows what failure is. The product is not for sale. Things only get worse after the reorganization. Deliveries are disrupted. The speaker is not applauded. The situation is getting out of control. A plot for a nightmare Everyone knows that failure is the opposite of success, and they improve the organization to protect themselves.

Layer by layer, management levels are built up to reduce risks and prevent disasters. It seems that if we narrow down the notion of failure, we take all actual events out of their scope, nothing threatens us, and there is nothing to panic about.

A manager's failure is often seen as the end, but it doesn't have to be. For most managers and their businesses, failure is just the beginning.

If you find that your business is sinking, it's time to change direction and find a solution to the problem. Just know that failure is a possibility.

Maybe you need to start over from the beginning. If so, fine. My own first business was a failure, but I'm still here (to say the least).

Why? Because I looked at the problems I had with my first company and used what I learned in my future decisions.

The 3Fs of Failure

If you have never had a failure (in business), you're probably living too comfortably a life and not taking enough risks. Alexandre Taillefer, serial entrepreneur

If you fail in high school and are usually graded an F, the same is true of business.

Depending on whom you ask, there are many reasons why management fails.

Each strand of management's DNA contributes its reasons for failure, but all relate directly to one of the 3 Fs.

1. Founder failures
3. Funding failures
4. Flawed business models

You can't tackle an issue you don't acknowledge or deny exists.

Understanding and acknowledging why management fails is crucial to their success. It enables you to create a strategy.

When I ask managers why their businesses fail, some show some knowledge, but many have never considered it. Managers who have a lot of fire and enthusiasm can be motivating, but their idealism can make them forget about the most common causes of failure, which can make things worse.

Founder (Manager)-Driven Failure

Managers are the lifeblood of any business and play a significant role in its success or failure. If I asked you to imagine a business manager, you would most likely think of Steve Jobs or Mark Zuckerberg, but these individuals are the exception rather than the rule.

Of course, business managers are as diverse as the concepts they build on. More than 450 million managers are believed to be working on the business in some form or another worldwide, with more joining the community every day.

These new managers are frequently unprepared for their trips. They mix up capacity with capability, and they'll need both to develop a successful business.

The ability of a manager to confront the day-to-day challenges of running and leading a business is referred to as founder capacity. This encompasses everything from physical fitness to mental and emotional preparedness.

Capacity is analogous to the fuel in your tank that permits you to travel. I see many managers having problems because they haven't spent enough time working on their capacity. This means that they haven't taken care of or developed themselves enough.

On the other hand, manager capability is more easily quantifiable and includes all the talents required to run a business.

Technical, communication, leadership, negotiation, and conflict resolution abilities are all included. Capacity is a lot easier to build than capability, but I think it's important for people to have the power to be successful.

Co-managers, or teams of co-managers, with complementary skills, are also more successful than single managers. Despite this, I've seen many firms fail due to a lack of cohesion among the managers. It's crucial to pick a co-manager and learn how to work with them.

Surrounding yourself with the appropriate people—from board members to advisers—will also help you achieve your goals.

Funding-Driven Failure

Failure owing to a lack of funds appears to be a foregone conclusion. Regardless of the primary cause of failure, most failed firms eventually run out of money.

This could be due to a lack of investor confidence in the managers or a failure to show the business plan. The deadly pinch comes at some point, and there isn't enough time to get new money before the company's cash reserves run out.

Surprisingly, a business might also fail due to excessive funding. Overfunded firms risk losing their competitive advantage and hustling. Giving a starving person a large supper and leading them to die from overeating is a good analogy.

Several well-funded companies have taken a step back, focusing on the new office fit-out and the design of their business cards rather than continuing to test their consumer hypotheses and value propositions.

Early-stage businesses, in my experience, have a fundraising sweet spot.

Discord between managers and investors can be just as damaging to a business. A business and its managers can do without investors breathing over their necks every step of the way or being mismatched for its future course. You must find the right investors and bring them along on the journey with you.

A Flawed Business Model

A business model is frequently confused by managers with a concept or a product. It's simple to fall in love with an idea, and it's even simpler to fall in love with a product. Ideas are inexpensive and plentiful!

Most businesses begin with a concept, which isn't always negative. On the other hand, most managers place far too much emphasis on that idea.

Business models, not ideas, are what make successful businesses. It's simple to come up with a clever idea, but it's more challenging to develop a full-fledged, profitable company plan.

There is a market for most ideas, but even that must be proven in many cases.

There are four types of business model failure:

- **Lack of desirability:** This is due to a lack of understanding of the problem and the solution the target client does not consider relevant.

- **Lack of feasibility:** Numerous reasons for a business's failure to execute. It could be due to bad recruiting, a focus on the wrong activities, or a lack of execution.

- **Lack of viability:** Concerning the critical income, growth rates, and expenses, it's crucial to manage cash burn within a business strategy that eventually leads to break-even and profitability. The investor community has recently shifted away from growth businesses (businesses that solely focus on user growth or other growth measures—think Twitter) and yield businesses (companies that focus on financial metrics like break-even and customer acquisition cost; think Google).

- **Lack of adaptability:** by definition, businesses are disruptive, but that doesn't mean they can't compete. It's essential to think about things like government regulation in remarkably regulated industries, as well as internal risks.

Deciding How to Decide

What motivates us to do what we do must be more important than failure. Then it will be possible to get up in a bit of time.

Safe Strategies

Is it possible to avoid this and try to live a life (at least a professional one) avoiding mistakes and defeats? Maybe success is not the conquest of some incredible peak but a series of successful, repetitive, proven movements. And it is better to do what is already well done, sit still, and not suffer from failure.

But only the "do not change anything" strategy seems safer at first glance. After all, any new movement brings the system out of balance and increases the risk of losing what is already there. By the way, this is the most common reason why management starts failing: people are afraid that, as a result, they will only worsen their position. Not just to suffer a public defeat (which in itself is already very unpleasant), but also to roll back several steps as a result of this defeat.

Comparative Risks

Why do some people still take risks? Because they are unique and not afraid of failure. The answer is not so obvious: they are better at assessing threats.

Stability, alas, is a dreadful thing—while we stand still, time passes, the world changes; there are new ideas, new idols, new values, and social norms. As a result, any attempt to freeze leads to a sad result: you become obsolete, and those who make decisions to act, abandon, and rebuild are simply choosing the strategy with the least risk.

Of course, they are also afraid of failure. Even those we think are the lucky ones who don't know the word "failure" either, they know, but they treat defeat not as the end of the route but as the next stage of the path—inevitable and valuable.

Helpful Mistakes

Today, no one believes in booming success. No one thinks of those who make mistakes and admit them as weak. Errors are no longer demonized. They are very carefully looked at with a microscope, and each one yields a lot of interesting findings.

Today, a person who cannot talk about their failed experience will not get through serious interviews. And it will not be of interest to either investors or partners. Today, even a business is much easier to get investments for if it already has several attempts under its belt, and even well, if unsuccessful.

Because behind every mistake and failure, there is an invaluable experience and something more important: resilience. So, when the bonds begin to crumble around you, all the calculations will turn out to be wrong, the market will collapse due to an unpredictable virus, and investors will take their money elsewhere, but you will remain on your feet. Try to find a new meaning in everything that happens after you have already had it all many times.

Small Failures Are Necessary to Avoid A Major Failure

The perception of failure in the business world is less severe since the movements supporting innovation and entrepreneurship advocate small, quick losses, the objective of which is to learn the complex reality through action and adapt.

It's not about rushing headlong.

For example, an entrepreneur who launches a new watch for cyclists will have to quickly test their idea through a few prototypes with their potential customers. It all depends on what people say and how happy they are with their products and business model. For example, they will know what kind of heart rate sensor to offer and how much it costs.

Let's imagine that the watch does not include geolocation but that 80% of the targeted cyclists want to know how fast they have traveled certain sections of their journey; this is a failure because we cannot meet customer expectations. But this is a minor failure that only concerns prototypes and will avoid a more significant loss: ending up with thousands of unsellable watches since they don't meet customer needs and no more dollars on hand.

Failure? Yes, but not just any!

Failure as A Springboard

In a situation of failure, possibilities that were not considered may appear. In this situation, open-mindedness and letting go will perhaps lead to results that exceed the objectives set. In an excellent mental context, failure can therefore lead to success. The loss of others can also serve as a springboard: participate in conferences, read testimonials, etc. Many analyses, such as "The X lessons we learn from the failure of businesses are also a resource on which to capitalize."

The Post-Mortem Way to Learn from Failure

At the very least, you're doing it incorrectly. Once you do, you have a chance to upgrade it. "Waiting for perfection is tantamount to not starting." - Seth Godin.

You can take advantage of your failures on the condition of not adopting the ostrich policy: knowing how to bounce back and develop learning that will be useful later. They are ways of making helpful failure, in a logic of trial-error-improvement.

This means taking the time to analyze the failure. Tools have been specially developed for the world of business.

But we can still look at the situation with a tool that many people don't use, but it's simple and very flexible: the post-mortem.

The post-mortem must be prepared to be helpful. It must occur while the situation is fresh in people's minds, but people must have had enough time to gather information. The content of a post-mortem can be very factual. For example, a reminder of the project, role of each, what worked well, what could have been done better, lessons learned, and actions to be taken. But it can also be very personal and subjective, a bit like a diary to take stock of how you feel about failure. This summary document will help me remember lessons when a similar project.

The Feeling of Failure

Failure is not pleasant. But it opens a window on reality, allows us to deploy our abilities or to get closer to our quest, our deep desire". Charles Pépin, philosopher and writer.

Whether a goal is achieved is subjective since it is linked to perception and emotions. When it comes to failure, to being in a mindset that is conducive to resilience, the critical question for a manager (for anyone, in fact) is:

- **Ownership of objectives:** is the manager convinced that the goals are achievable? What impact do these objectives have on its mission and vision? Does the manager find them relevant and desirable? Did the manager set these goals themselves, or did others impose them? Are these people essential and credible?

- **Responsibility:** what factors caused the failure? Were they controllable by the contractor? What is the manager's share of responsibility for the loss? What could they have done differently? Do they manage to let go, or are they overwhelmed by guilt? etc.

- **Social pressure:** how does the manager's entourage perceive failure? Does society tolerate failure? Is the opinion of others significant to the manager? What is the contractor's reputation?

The power to learn

What doesn't kill me makes me stronger.

Accept Failure

Failure is part of the process of creating a business and being a manager.

You may have heard many reports of "overnight success." In most cases, these stories hide the mistakes behind these achievements.

For example, doctors and researchers often create thousands of vaccines that don't work until they come up with one that does.

In the same way, managers sometimes create many businesses until they find a formula that results in profits.

On the other hand, some managers are so afraid of failure that they become paralyzed. And that fear prevents them from taking action, changing direction, and creating.

If you are afraid of failure, try to learn to accept it. You are not the only one.

Be Honest

Let's say your company or a specific product is a failure. In the business world, you need to be honest with your team.

If your business starts to lose momentum or if you've made a severe mistake, admit it.

Managers often feel alone in building their companies and also in their failures. But you are not alone. Your team and partners are with you through success or failure.

The sooner you admit a problem, the more likely they will want to help you solve the problem and persist in making your business a success.

Many managers and business people feel uncertain about their future.

If you don't admit your failure, someone will point it out. If someone else has to point out your mistake or loss, the situation will look much worse.

It's much better to be direct and honest when you have made a mistake or even bankrupted your business.

Of course, you also need to be honest with yourself.

Don't lie to yourself that there isn't a problem when you know you have one. Early detection of a problem can mean you'll have plenty of time to fix it.

The alternative is to have a massive mess on your hands.

Answer Questions

If you fail at something, the consequences don't just fall on you, but on your team as well. After admitting your mistake, you can offer explanations but no excuses.

If you admit your mistake and publicly examine it, you'll learn more about what went wrong.

Also, asking and answering questions is part of examining failure. You should also feel comfortable answering any questions your team might have.

Instead of hiding in your office, set up a meeting. Instead of pretending you're swimming in cash, show your team a profit and loss spreadsheet.

Your honesty and willingness to answer questions will strengthen your team's group mindset. And from there, you can start rebuilding.

Businesses are naturally resistant to failure, as they can easily change direction. This gives them some advantages over the big companies and the potential to beat even their biggest competitors.

Deal with Your Emotions

There is a big difference between a reaction and a response.

The reaction is your emotional and automatic response. It usually adds to the problem.

This is because business is not an emotional area. The stock exchange doesn't care whether you're making money or not. Neither do your customers.

An emotional reaction leads to a lack of movement and action.

On the other hand, a response implies overcoming inertia.

For example, if you know your leads aren't converting, you can adjust your marketing funnel to attract lost potential customers.

Likewise, if your products don't resonate with your consumers, you can go back to the development phase.

By examining and dealing with your emotions, you will be more likely to respond to failure rather than simply react to it.

Dealing with your emotions doesn't mean ignoring them. A manager's failure can lead to anger, sadness, fear, or other negative feelings.

Examine these emotions. Take some time to process what happened and create a plan to make positive changes.

Learn It

The idea is straightforward: learn from your failures. Regardless of what the problem was, there is always something you can learn from the experience of loss.

An essential part of turning failure into an advantage is learning how and why the loss happened.

Failure to learn from failure leaves the door open for more losses in the future. As a manager, you may often make mistakes.

However, if you don't take this opportunity to grow and rebuild, you will never experience the joyous moments of having your own business.

Start from scratch. I have a new idea. Get excited about something you are passionate about.

Knowing that many new businesses fail prevents many people from starting small businesses.

Don't let the possibility of failure stop you from achieving your dreams. Accept that the future is uncertain and that failure is a possibility.

Plan for the future.
An essential part of learning from failure involves making plans for the future. Making the same mistake means you didn't learn from it.

Almost 30% of businesses fail due to a lack of money. Many are funded externally, but 79% of small businesses with fewer than five employees also use their manager(s) resources, which is decreasing.

Your plan will change over time. But not having a plan is a failure in itself.

Planning for the future allows you to have extra capital, an emergency plan, and a solid team to anticipate potential problems and keep good momentum.

Get Motivated

Transform the anxiety generated by failure into motivation.

Failure is just one step on the long journey to success as a manager. Use it as motivation to make your business a hit instead of making you afraid to submit to it.

The combination of failure and fear can be the end of your business. But when combined with motivation, failure by managers can lead to success.

Suppose you need to find motivation when things fail; remember everyone who told you couldn't. And then get up and go on your way.

Gain Perspective

Just as you can use failure as motivation, use it to gain perspective.

Failure means you tried something. If you had never created a business, you could not have failed at it. Use this perspective to address your future goals and obstacles.

Failure can show you what your weaknesses are.

Examine your failures to find your business' weaknesses.

Did you have trouble generating brand recognition? Do your customers have difficulty finding you on the internet?

Once you've identified these weaknesses, you can test new ideas. I love creating hypotheses and testing them in real life.

If you don't know how to gain perspective on your failure, ask for help. Asking an outside source or mentor to look over your business when there is a failure can be very helpful in gaining perspective.

You may not gain perspective right away. Processing failure, letting go of emotions, and getting back to thinking logically can take a lot of time.

Once you can think logically, you can gain the perspective you need to turn around your business gone wrong.

Avoid Burnout

Managers often feel like hamsters on a wheel: running in circles, getting nowhere.

Don't let the failure of your business wear you out.

Burnout is prevalent in the world of management. Businesses require many hours of work and a total commitment to their managers. It is straightforward to exhaust your resources working like this.

Instead of continuing to run like a hamster, stop for a moment and assess the direction you are heading. Repeating the same action several times will not change its result.

When you're stuck, try the opposite approach. Many managers come up with their best ideas when they revisit a problem and think about other ways to solve it.

By using their own money, these managers invest everything in their business. This often means that the whole family is invested in that company.

This creates a lot of pressure!
So, deep immersion in your business in terms of time and money can make it easy to burn out if you ignore the warning signs.

High levels of stress, lack of sleep, and lack of clarity are symptoms of burnout.

You don't want to lose momentum. You can overcome your flaws instead of letting them dominate you and ruin your business.

We Have Had Many Setbacks
Everything or nothing. This is the motto of many managers.

Myself included.

And that doesn't just apply to success. Think big and create something huge if you are starting a new business.

A big failure means that you have the potential to be a big success. If you can fail, you lose nothing in doing something great.

A big failure can be used to your advantage, just as a slight loss can be. Maybe you just need more time to figure out what to do next.

A big failure can be the end of your current business, but it doesn't mean you're out of the game.

I have already created several companies. Some are bigger hits than others. And as I mentioned, I've failed several times.

Does this mean I should settle for a life of unfulfilled dreams? Of course not!

When failure is big, you know the attempt was significant too.

Fail Quickly

If you are going to fail, do it quickly. A slow drop isn't going to reduce the pain when you finally hit rock bottom.

When you realize your business is failing, it's time to respond aggressively. The faster you can adjust your strategy, the quicker you can succeed.

Take Advantage of Failure

Failure is an excellent time to review your objectives and stakeholders' objectives in your managerial approach. Indeed, co-managers, customers, investors, suppliers, etc., do not necessarily share the same goals. Everyone sets their own goals and perceives failure both according to their interests and those of the group. It is, therefore, necessary to understand and agree on the objectives set out and the motivations of each.

It is also necessary to communicate the mission of the project and the vision so that the actions and means are aligned in a common direction. Does the end justify the means? Success can have a bitter taste if the standards do not align with the manager and stakeholders' motivations, values, and philosophy.

In conclusion, failure is increasingly perceived as a situation conducive to improvement if we know how to fail, get up, analyze it, and take the necessary actions to capitalize on it.

We must develop "failed management" through learning and resilience.

Dare! Fall! Then get up! And go on!

ECCO

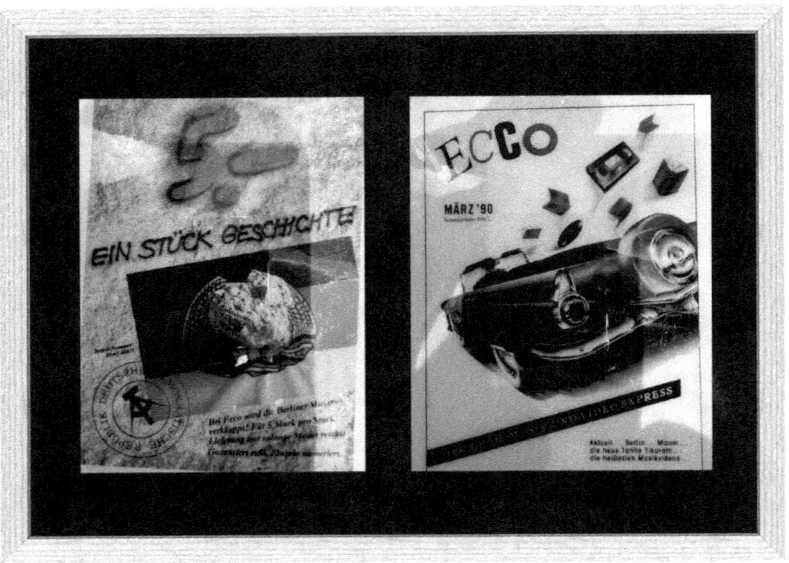

Chapter 5

ROAMING INSIDE THE BOX

The accelerated aging of the population, the economic crisis, global competition, and global problems create an environment that requires more managers to demonstrate courage and critical leadership skills.

I'm not just talking about courage in the sense of heroes. I'm talking about the courage to think outside the box, innovate more, take more risks, step out of our comfort zone, and sometimes make difficult decisions.

Boxes and Innovative Decisions

As we all know, innovating and creating something new is usually viewed, and rightly so, as a big but very risky endeavor. As such, those responsible for innovation are under constant pressure from all sides.

When the subject of innovation is discussed, we often focus on the practical aspects of the subject, such as processes, best practices, and tools. These are undoubtedly critical topics, but they pale in comparison to decision-making.

If innovation decision-making is flawed in a company, no gimmick will make a real difference. And unfortunately, this is an area where many, if not most, business managers struggle.

Why Is It So Hard to Make Smart Innovation Decisions?
Let's start by looking at the main characteristics of innovation.

By definition, it's about doing something new that has never been done before. Consequently, there is a lot of uncertainty and question marks attached to almost everything new or different, so this is how it is.

In many cases, you are also working to solve problems in a complex environment, which means that things are intertwined and, therefore, it is difficult to predict what will happen.

Due to the above, there is usually not much historical data to rely on.

There are also no reliable benchmarks or market studies available. And, since everything is new, the data you can get from customer questionnaires/surveys or other similar methods probably won't be reliable either.

Also, since your team has never done this before, you can't create a very realistic project plan to implement it.

When you put it all together, you end up in a challenging environment to manage, and in most cases, you won't have the data you need to make evidence-based decisions or realistic plans.

The Lure of The Exciting and The New

Going deeper by comparing innovation decision-making with the context of "ordinary" decision-making

In any given company, most managers get where they are because they were successful in what the company did in the past. And as they have risen to leadership positions, they have a great responsibility for the company and a lot to lose on a personal level.

This means they want to make informed, evidence-based decisions with the lowest possible risk and the highest possible return. They want to have a well-thought-out and structured plan ahead of time, allocate resources accordingly, and closely monitor progress against the roadmap while continuously improving the process.

And for a good reason, not wanting to do this would be simply reckless or just plain stupid!

However, the problem is that, because they have a way of operating on their own, they are used to having a lot of data, most of which is quite reliable. Sometimes, there is also a history of how the collaborators have done in the missions they have been given. This makes it possible to make plans set way into the future.

As we've already said, none of the above is possible for new ideas, or at least not in the real world!

Innovation takes place in an extensive context. To be good at it, the "innovators" need to understand these critical differences between creation and its history and then change their thinking to fit them.

This is, of course, easier said than done when you've had plenty of success working the other way around for years, even decades.

The Art of Deciding the Right Things

As we just learned, innovation leaders must be quick to make many decisions in an environment with many risks.

So, while it's essential to be decisive, uncertainty also means you will have to be comfortable putting off certain decisions, leaving questions open.

The skill that the best innovators master is determining which questions should be addressed now and which should be left open. They ask the right questions and focus on making the right decisions, not just the questions and findings presented to them.

The best innovators ask the right questions and focus on making the right decisions, not just the questions and findings presented to them.

To explain what this means, let's use a somewhat oversimplified example that isn't related to innovation per se, but one that we can all relate to:

You often hear people say that you can either work hard or work smart, and then you have to decide which of the two you want them to do.

The question is a trap because no one wants to "work dumb," so of the options presented, all you can do is say is "work smart." But that's the wrong answer.

By simply choosing one or the other, whichever one you choose, you will never get great results. To contact them, of course, you have to work both hard and smart.

So, the real question is: how to change the system so that you don't have to choose between one or the other, but can have both?

As a manager, you must ignore these irrelevant choices that people often use as excuses to choose the path of least resistance. Try to dig deeper and find answers to the questions that matter.

This is how actual managers and innovators think: they find ways to change the system to get the results.

This is how actual managers and innovators think: they find ways to change the system to achieve their desired outcome.

This is, of course, easier said than done!

However, the world is filled with situations and decisions like this one, where you have to choose between less-than-ideal alternatives. In some cases, you can select one or the other, but for the questions and issues that matter, you can't settle for these mediocre, at best, options and results.

The only way to get past these options and get great results is to ask the question that most people haven't asked yet, or at least haven't been able to answer.

Examples of Misleading Choices in Practice
There are countless examples of this phenomenon in leadership and innovation. Here are some common examples:

- "Do you want it done rightly (reliably, safely…), or do you want it done quick"y"""

- "Do you want incremental innovation or disruptive innovati"n"""

- "Do you want to lead by example or empower your te"m?"

The answer to these questions is never one or the other, but always both. The exact balance between the two extremes will be different in each situation, but the results will not be the same if you choose only one or the other.

Thinking Outside the Box

All of this can make it seem nearly impossible to make intelligent innovation decisions.

The good news is that it do'sn't, provided you understand a few basics. As long as you act on them, 'ou'll most likely make the right choices. This do'sn't guarantee innovation success, of course, but it does go a long way to improving your chances of success.

1. Accept that your strategy and business plans are always wrong.

The first and most important thing is that you have to accept that whatever innovation strategy or business plan you have created will always be completely wrong or, at best, understated. A common saying in the business world sums it up nicely: "No business plan survives the first contact with a client."

To sum up, it's essential to understand that if 'ou're innovating, 'ou're constantly pushing boundaries and exploring the unknown. As such, you will never be able to see everything clearly, nor have all the answers in advance.' It's just something that successful innovators have learned to organize their time wisely. You still need goals and a strategy, and it's always helpful to have plans, but you have to accept that there are many flaws in them. So, there is no point in spending a lot of time trying to make them perfect. Instead, focus on finding their spots as quickly as possible. And the only way to do that is to put the plan into practice and adapt it accordingly promptly.

This fundamental cornerstone leads to our following vital points: test, learn, adapt, progress.

2. Test your plan quickly—and start with the riskiest parts. As we have just seen, once you accept that your plan is wrong, the real work is no longer to ensure that the program is followed to the letter. It's about testing the initial plan, whatever it is, with the goal of learning which parts work and, more importantly, which ones don't, and then adapting them accordingly.

Too many managers may sound unsophisticated and unscientific, but they are not.

Let's go back to what those of us who have taken a university course have learned: the scientific method. The idea is to start with a theory or hypothesis, then carry out field tests to verify this hypothesis and analyze the results to see if it is correct. That's how you do cutting-edge research, and that's also how you innovate, pure and simple.

So, as a business manager or decision-maker, remember that your strategy, as well as your business plan and market research, are only hypotheses waiting to be tested. The real work, and the difference between those who fail and those who succeed, will be your ability to adapt to everything you learn— fast enough and well enough.

The key to doing this may be counter-intuitive for many of us: we have to start with the riskiest assumption.

In most business ventures, it makes sense to get quick results first to get things done and gain support, but for strategy and innovation, it's usually problematic.

In many cases, this leads to a false sense of accomplishment because you set small goals when there is always a bigger goal in sight.

Result: You work a lot and spend a lot of money only to realize that the original plan won't work without significant changes when you encounter this challenge.

At that point, most of that hard work will have to be thrown away, and you will have wasted a lot of time in the process as well. Or worse, you risk falling prey to a sunk cost error and continuing with no real chance of success.

On the other hand, if you start by testing the riskiest and most critical part, you will probably experience difficulties and failures at first. Still, you will soon reach a point where you understand the problem well enough to solve it in the right way.

This will save you time and money later on and minimize the risk of the project ending in a highly costly failure.

For most companies, the riskiest parts are usually related to customer demand, but there are also cases where it can be different, such as technology.

For example, if you develop a super effective and affordable cure for all kinds of cancers, the rest is insignificant. There will be no shortage of demand, and it will not be challenging to build a great business from there. In this case, you should focus on solving the technical challenge and not worry too much about marketing, distribution channels, etc.

On the other hand, in the 21st century, it is easy to create the following social media platform. You can do this as an individual with little to no prior coding experience and a minimal budget. The big question is whether anyone will want to use it or pay for it. So, it doesn't make sense to tweak every aspect of the platform and get it ready for a massive launch across all distribution platforms at once if you don't have solid evidence of demand for what you're doing.

3. Focus on speed—today's wrong decision is better than a good one later.

The third and final key to successful innovation decision-making is to focus on the speed of decision-making. In many large companies, decision-making tends to be relatively slow. It is often helpful to seek input from all parts of the organization on a potential decision and have them sign off on it ahead of time to reduce resistance to change along the way and avoid having to take personal responsibility for bad choices.

And since most decision-makers are very busy, it can take weeks or even months to contact them all, update them and provide enough information for them to approve a decision, even if it is relatively simple. As we mentioned, there is, of course, an interest in doing it this way, but even with all this information, decisions will often be wrong when it comes to innovation for the reasons we have already discussed. In the end, this value will be relatively marginal compared to the whole.

However, the cost of this type of slow, participatory decision-making is enormous, both in terms of working time and lost calendar slots. Also, innovations are almost always controversial, and if a consensus has to be reached, chances are you'll end up with a worse, watered-down version of the original idea.

Couple this with the fact that many, if not most, initial decisions, much like business plans, will be less than optimal anyway due to high uncertainty, and it's best to make a quick decision even if it's worse now than trying to make a seemingly perfect decision later.

If you act quickly and decisively, you can usually make the right decision, implement it, and know if it was the right one in the time it takes some organizations to make that decision. This is a critical competitive advantage nearly impossible for a slower organization to overcome.

So, when it comes to innovation, always prioritize action. Don't wait for more information or more advice; just take action and make sure you're moving in the right general direction, even if you have to sort out some details as you go along.

By understanding and applying these three fundamental principles in your decision-making, you will do better than most other organizations.

However, the best innovation managers go beyond these fundamentals.

The power of common sense

In conclusion, working on innovation requires a different mindset than most of us are used to. As such, it's often difficult for organizations to make intelligent decisions about innovation, and even if you succeed, you may also need to change the views of those around you.

This is one of the main reasons many people and organizations fail regarding innovation.

Remember that a poor decision now is always better than a good decision later—and be sure to focus on the decisions that matter, not the ones people throw at you. That's what "thinking outside the box" really means.

If you can change your mindset and improve your decision-making skills to be better prepared to deal with uncertainty and complexity, you will succeed in innovation and life!

Come on, dare!

Chapter 6

OLD SCHOOL MANAGEMENT

You are in the ICU, on a tightrope between staying or being laid off at the company where you work, and still have a lot of important work to do. The manager comes in and says, "We have two employees here who can help you." One has been with us for years and knows everything. Not cool!

The other is a beginner; they're still learning. But it would be nice for them to take a job of great importance to gain experience. Which one do you prefer?

As dynamic as you are, you want to make quick decisions on everything. Then choose the most experienced.

Well, you know that you made the wrong choice. Some recent studies show that experience is not as necessary as everyone thinks. It can even hinder performance, at least in new situations. Administration, nursing, diplomacy, volleyball, or the country's presidency are all jobs that require unexpected things to happen, so it doesn't matter what kind of job you have.

More thought-provoking research on the subject by neuroscientists at the University of Florida involved both novice and veteran nurses dealing with dying patients. It was a robot programmed to alternate symptoms like high, low, and tachycardia—and to die if you took the wrong medicine at the wrong time. A severe case, and that's what happened to the nurses. All of them let the virtual patient die. But this was not a surprise. Some novices managed to keep the doll alive longer than experienced ones.

Why? Simple enough. Veterans relied heavily on instinct, disregarding basic information about changes in the patient's condition, and, despite acting faster than new ones, they were wrong more quickly as well. There is confirmation that most drowned people are people who know how to swim. Therefore, confidence is essential, but with responsibility.

The experience is not a bad thing. It is essential, especially in decision-making. It is proven that the most experienced decide better, while the novices are excellent performers. We can cite a classic example: The great chess players (international masters of the board) can remember the position of more or less 25 pieces of a game that they have just played, while the beginners only have 4. The problem is when something unforeseen happens-if, you randomly place pieces on a board; masters are almost as "lost" as beginners when it comes to remembering their position.

Managers need to be good listeners and pay attention to small details and information, even though listening is at the heart of improvisation, which means that managers need to be good listeners.

The Battle Within

The problem of professional development of managers today is more acute than ever: to survive in an unstable, unreliable, complex, and contradictory business environment, leaders need to master new skills, and organizations need to accumulate new potential. There is a growing understanding in business circles that it is not only top managers and their associates that need to be trained in management.

With the development of collaborative platforms for solving problems, where participants have equal rights and initiative is encouraged, an increasing number of employees at different levels begin to take responsibility within corporate strategy and culture. They must have the required technical, team, and communication skills.

The executive education industry, however, is not in the best shape. More and more players in this market offer to teach technical and social skills to managers. Still, businesses that spend several billion dollars a year training current and future managers are less and less satisfied with the results. Several large-scale studies confirmed what we already knew from conversations with clients: more than half of company managers believe that their efforts to develop talent do not lead to the emergence of critical skills and organizational competencies.

We see three main reasons for failure. First of all, this is a discrepancy in motivation: organizations invest in the training of managers, assuming long-term benefits for themselves, and those who participate in programs for their development and career growth often leave the company that paid for their training. The second inconsistency is that the skills taught by development programs are not always applied. This is especially true of interpersonal communication, essential in today's flat, closely knit organizations. Old school training providers are excellent at teaching and evaluating cognitive skills, but they lack experience in developing communication and teamwork skills. Finally, the third inconsistency concerns the use of skills.

Simply put, not all managers apply what they have learned at work. The farther the acquisition of knowledge is in place and time from its application, the greater the inconsistency. To effectively train leaders and managers, organizations must overcome these three gaps.

Problems with Old School Management

Learning managers argue that old-school programs can no longer prepare managers for current and future challenges. Companies need people with communication skills and the ability to influence, anticipate, and direct teams that work closely with each other. At the same time, most educational programs for top managers focus on technical skills such as strategy development and financial analysis and do not pay enough attention to social and interpersonal skills. It's no wonder that directors of learning have a hard time justifying the money they spend on training.

Programs for top managers do not cope even with their direct tasks. "Lifelong learning" has been discussed in corporate and academia for decades, but it remains a dream. At the same time, old-school education remains too episodic, exclusive, and expensive. Not surprisingly, top business schools like Rothman and Harvard are seeing an explosion in demand for personalized group programs that target the talent development needs of specific firms.

The existing gaps are beginning to be filled by corporate universities and the personal learning cloud, creating their own sets of online courses, social and interactive platforms, and learning tools used by both old-timers and newcomers to the business education market.

Standing in The Way

Every business starts small, and, understandably, not everything is perfect; the company is under construction. Along with this organized chaos, there are attitudes that managers must adopt and others that they must avoid in the workplace. My experience as an entrepreneur and a startup employee helped me identify pain points regarding employee motivation.

1. Having no vision

Failing to provide vision reveals the pilot does not know where the plane is heading. Even when the business doesn't know how to generate money, everyone needs to understand why they are coming to work every morning; they need to know where all these tasks are leading them.

Your early employees may understand the lack of vision, as researching a business model can be time-consuming and tedious. Once found, the vision and mission should be the top priorities on the manager's to-do list. Indeed, all employees must work toward the same goal, and the company is in charge of coming up with and explaining this mission.

2. Not knowing who your employees are and their intrinsic values.

Knowing your employees, especially if you don't have a thousand of them, and their intrinsic values give you a good understanding of who they are and how they behave. This will provide you with the keys to ad hoc management and allow your company to develop great cohesion. A simple action to get to know your employees is to eat with them at least once a week and ask fundamental questions to show a sincere interest in their lives.

Failing on this will slowly lead you to create a collection of individuals and ultimately never create a team that can scale and grow together. Failing to be close to your employees will also cause you to keep what you know to yourself and quietly cut off communication so much that you won't be able to listen to them when they have something important to tell you.

3. It also breeds mistrust and disrespect.

Failing to reward initiative (good or bad) and assuming that people always make bad decisions will gradually lead your teams to mistrust and disengagement. Saying no or being harmful to every question undermines morale and undermines good ideas. You kill motivation, and fewer and fewer people will ask you. This will create a distance between you and the employees (because they believe in you and the company). They will fear you and think that you are useless because you have failed to help them achieve their professional goals.

There is also another type of devaluation, such as not listening to your employees during meetings (being on your phone or doing something else) or canceling appointments at the last moment without warning, reason, and follow-up.

Especially when you know people have been waiting for you, specifically for a long time.

This is one of the best ways to kill motivation, much better than refusing a raise, which is nevertheless perceived as the culmination of all these "invisible" actions.

4. Not involving employees

From a business perspective, keeping too much information in the hands of just a few employees can lead to global mistrust. Employees go to work because they want to contribute to a mission and leave an imprint. If you don't involve people, they will think they don't belong and gradually become demotivated. When you hire someone, consider them valuable and trustworthy from the start; otherwise, what are they doing there?

5. Not setting reachable goals for your employees

Is everyone familiar with SMART goals?

- S-Specific
- M-Measurable
- A-Accessible
- R-Realistic
- T-Temporal

Simple enough, right?

Each objective or task must respect this structure. Managers ignore this simple canvas. If you want your employees to be demotivated quickly, don't even set a goal or, even worse, tell them that they didn't achieve the goals you didn't set. Success is guaranteed!

6. Let ambiguous situations rot.

Ambiguous situations can be multiple: technical debts or exemptions granted to someone when the company has only two employees. Every business has what I call a "moment of structuring" where things have to scale and, for that, the foundations have to be solid. This is when the manager must put in place rules and good practices to steer the team in the right direction with the proper means.

Doing so allows for creating a work environment that is hard and stimulating so that employees work hard and give their best.

7. I am not defining values or governance.

It is considered normal not to have organized governance in the company's early months or even years because the managers make most of the decisions. Often, business rites have been driven by them.

Employees arriving, governance and rituals may become unsuitable because they were thought of in another era. Moreover, corporate culture has often not been imagined or written and its intrinsic values. It's about creating governance that sticks to your business, with different points of view, and not just listening to the most charismatic person or the one who speaks last.

Along with governance, create habits and rituals that make sense and involve everyone. When you are in the early stages, write your corporate values (even on a tablecloth at the restaurant) and do not hesitate to update them with your employees as you go. With this, you will lay the foundation for the corporate culture you and your employees deserve.

All this comes from the lack of a vision for the whole company because the image corresponds to the what, when, and why.

The governance, the rites, the culture, and the values are the how. You, your employees, and the ecosystem are the Who and Where.

Unfortunately, failing to answer these questions creates hazy management and, sooner or later, there will be a lack of cohesion in the company. It's better sooner than later!

8. The wrong people are being promoted.

Employees who arrived at the start of the project often gained trust by getting involved in projects for which they had to expose themselves and step out of their trust zone. They acquired their status little by little.

Newcomers must also climb the ladder step by step. To do the opposite is to send the message that the place of the "elders" was due to a simple combination of circumstances and that trust can be earned quickly without great effort. It demotivates alumni, creates dissension, and can kill an employee's ability to give back to the company. It is thought to be unfair, and newcomers will one day take the place of the old ones and feel the same way, which is terrible for the company.

This correlates with not knowing your employees well enough. Give yourself time to discover their personalities. In addition, the implicit message sent to all of your employees is that trust is more important and that you recognize efforts at their actual value.

Your employees do not all share the same point of view. Some will follow you; some won't. But like-minded people will be amazed if you reward "negative people." This happens when managers are disconnected from the field. Finally, as you will have understood, this leads to a deep demotivation among "trustworthy people" and pushes them to leave.

9. Prioritize short-term profits over the long term

Indeed, it turns out that early-stage business managers are desperate to generate revenue, and they are right because the most important thing is to find those who want to pay for your product. But, when it's been months or even years since you found your business model and have scalable products, you have to think ahead of everyone else instead of worrying about immediate profits.

You would only gain additional time in your product roadmap to earn a tiny amount, and you would ruin the prospect of making a more considerable turnover in the next 6 to 12 months.

Suppose you let your employees prioritize short-term decisions over long-term decisions. In that case, the company will not develop new ideas and will not be able to work on long-term projects, which means that your best employees will leave.

10. We are not learning from mistakes.

Making mistakes is human, and no one will hold it against you, especially in business. But making the same mistakes twice is sending your employees a sign that nothing will change and that they won't get any further in this company.

Trustor Control?

Trust is often perceived as intangible and refers to a personal and qualitative feeling. Many managers prefer control to not needing to discern, evaluate, and feel trust. However, a leader who manages their employees as if they were children should not be surprised to have the impression of "running a daycare."

However, in the context of remote management and hybrid management, which require putting trust at the center of interactions between employees and their managers, the famous "plan, organize, direct, and control" (PODC) still has a place.

The very nature of the management profession remains the same. However, change is essential in "how" an employee or manager chooses to be and acts daily.

Organizational performance depends on the level of trust established and maintained between individuals, who will undoubtedly be scattered all over the planet or in precisely the exact physical locations. It remains essential to linger and invest in developing human skills to achieve this. Reflection will help us find and measure our level of confidence as often as we count our financial ratios, productivity indices, and the level of engagement of our troops.

Components of the Confidence Quotient
What should the confidence quotient be made of? Self-confidence, empathy, and benevolence, as well as the benefit of the doubt and the right to make mistakes,

- **The absolute confidence of each member of the organizational ecosystem**

Confidence breeds confidence. So, it's essential that the hiring criteria, like those used for promotions and internal transfers, the evaluation and remuneration systems, and the development plans, align with the desire to build and keep a culture of trust.

To do this, beyond technical expertise and the individual confidence it provides, it is now essential to measure the level of "real" confidence, i.e., the group that emanates from personal and individual development.

- **Empathy and caring in relationships and decision-making**

An organizational culture based on trust requires everyone to show compassion in their communications and interactions. Thus, by developing their ability to put themselves in the place of the other, the individual develops other reflexes than those of looking for a culprit and other habits than those of thinking that they're always right.

A decision-making system that encourages and promotes empathetic and caring behavior in relationships helps its ecosystem build the emotional security needed to work together and develop new ideas.

- **The benefit of the doubt and the right to make mistakes in judging one another**

Managers who wish to maintain a high trust quotient must avoid spending their energy managing the 10% of people who do not fully buy into the organizational culture and common purpose.

Instead, they must direct their attention to the 90% of people who, individually and collectively, want to succeed. These employees agree to evolve in a volatile, uncertain, complex, and ambiguous (VUCA) work environment. They are willing to take risks and make mistakes that will teach them how to learn.

Absolute individual confidence is strengthened by offering the right to make mistakes and developing empathy and benevolence in judging and evaluating. Suppose we multiply it by the number of people in the organization's ecosystem. In that case, we can change the culture of trust that is needed to improve business results over time and stay healthy.

The Step Up

The transformation of work in the age of digital globalization is accelerating. People are increasingly choosing to be their managers, and a growing number of businesses and freelancers are dealing through online platforms. In some areas of the business world, innovative strategies are emerging that focus on giving all employees greater freedom and choice about where and how they work.

I have discovered that companies implementing new work practices have a lot to gain. They benefit in particular from increased productivity, cost savings, faster access to new markets, expanded customer service, access to a larger pool of talent, and the continuation of activities, even in the event of disruption caused by significant events, such as hurricanes and earthquakes.

Major forces underpin this transformation of work, such as rapid advances in communications technology, globalization, changing workforce demographics, and the urgent need to address climate change.

However, the gap is widening between managers who are looking for the flexibility offered by the work of the future and companies that are struggling to break away from the old working practices of the industrial age, characterized by a fixed time and place of work and a management style based on control (or, at least, the illusion of control).

A successful transition to a 21st-century work model begins with recognizing the need to change organizational culture, leadership styles, and management attitudes. You may reorganize workspaces and modernize technology, but the real key to success will still be behavior change.

Based on the experiences of several pioneering companies making this transition, we have developed five principles to guide companies that want to adapt and thrive in the new world of work. They are grouped under the acronym "TRUST":

1. Trust your employees.
It is essential to trust your employees if you decide to grant them greater freedom to give the best of themselves. This trust must be reciprocal; managers and employees alike must adapt and be ready to take responsibility for setting and achieving clear objectives.

Many managers must learn, through practice, to detach themselves from this need to control, which is often their "default" mode of operation. They also need to challenge their misconceptions, such as thinking that an employee's presence in the workplace for long hours is a sign of their involvement.

Managers can demonstrate their confidence by encouraging their teams to achieve corporate goals more effectively and responding to individual preferences and needs. Those working in the field usually have a better view of how things can be improved. Managers who don't put many restrictions on their employees while giving them more freedom are the ones who will help their companies both be more motivated and be more productive.

2. Reward results, not hours.

The working model of the future is first and foremost about results. It is not the effort expended to accomplish a task that defines it, but its objective, and it is the latter's achievement that management must concern itself with. How goals are set and the results to be achieved will vary from sector to sector and from job to job.

Focusing purely and simply on the numbers can, in some cases, have harmful consequences. Broader goals, such as providing excellent customer service or ensuring patients are treated with compassion, are at least as necessary as targets.

For many knowledge workers, where they work is irrelevant. A growing number of options and places are available to them, from the office and home to innovative work platforms, cafes, libraries, and public transport. The challenge is increasingly finding the right place and time for the task at hand, whether it's meeting clients, writing a complex report, or collaborating online with an international team.

For managers, a great way to show that performance matters more than hours is to ensure that individual work patterns aren't considered for promotions. This sends a strong change signal to the rest of the organization.

3. Understand the business case.

Each time we found a company fully committed to implementing new working practices, it was driven by a business objective. Every business needs to develop a business plan, whether it's increasing productivity, preventing the loss of talent, adapting faster to new markets, or taking advantage of a technological edge.

Most progress has adopted a transversal strategy encompassing HR, finance, real estate, IT, and communication. This also makes it possible to measure the benefits to the company immediately. However, care must be taken not to see this as a simple cost-cutting measure, as it will be counterproductive if employees have nothing to gain from it.

4. Start at the top.

The future working model involves moving from management based on control to leadership based on trust and treating people like adults. This transformation will not be possible without the support of senior management. Senior leaders must be on board with this new model and talk about how important it is to balance flexibility and stability.

While many managers favor this approach and may already be doing it, they usually don't realize how important it is to talk about it. Indeed, the power of leadership is such that it can permit others to grow.

5. Treat people as individuals.

There is no one-size-fits-all solution for the future of work. Successful managers will understand their team members' different motivations and preferences and support everyone's needs. Managers should articulate their expectations clearly and ensure that working "anywhere, anytime" does not mean "everywhere, anytime." With geographically dispersed teams, managers must allow employees to communicate through "virtual coffee breaks" and invest in developing one-on-one relationships over the phone (or Skype) when it's not possible to meet physically.

Finally, it is essential to manage new ways of working. On the one hand, poor management can cause dissatisfaction and cut employees off from the organization and, on the other hand, cause burnout. The solution is not to go back to the old ways of working. Instead, it's about managers being better at setting goals and evaluating performance while motivating employees to reach their full potential, no matter where they work or how they work.

More seriously, think about putting people first; remember that your employees are people you have convinced to join you. Even if you trust the people you hire, they may fail from time to time, just like you and me, but know that they will do everything in their power to succeed. They are your only way to get where you want to go. Never forget that they chose to get up every morning to pursue your dream and grow your business.

These people are the key to your success.

ECCO

My-mindguide.com

Chapter 7

BAD MANAGEMENT HABITS

"Success is the ability to go from failure to failure without losing enthusiasm." - Winston Churchill

Bad habits can limit your potential; the more significant your conscious inability to perceive and understand yourself and your practices, the more difficult it will be to develop and perform.

There is a high level of temptation to get distracted and let bad habits stay in your life, which can significantly impact your mindset (mental model) and how you see and interpret the world. This can keep your perspective from being calibrated or updated.

We imagine that we are in control, using our rational minds for all day-to-day decisions. Unfortunately, this is not true: we follow many automatic habits, and the worst one is spending more energy doing less.

Habits influence our actions, including how we behave with our employees. In business, no one is immune to failure.

Running a business and the leading team is a very delicate mission. Your behavior is the cornerstone of your employees' involvement. Successful entrepreneurs have some habits that separate them from those who don't work out.

Sometimes, when work stops, managers are unaware that employees have lost the motivation to continue. And all because of the sudden intervention of the manager in the process! But who, if not the leader, should manage and control the process? And why are employees offended if the manager, interfering, fulfill their direct duties? However, these bad habits of managers do hinder achieving results for employees. Let's talk about them.

Miscommunication and Not Listening to Others

Poor communication skills or even the total absence of communication within the team is one of the leading causes of management failure. A section that does not communicate will lock itself in and withdraw into itself. Adverse effects can be seen in the project's progress and success when the atmosphere in the workplace changes.

You have convictions when you're a business manager, and you don't want to waste a minute. Other, more effective ways of acting could appear to you by listening to others. Unfortunately, it is common to realize that we no longer listen to others. Very often, taking the time to bring a bath of youth to your ideas, which are undoubtedly judicious but need to be innovative, must be the subject of honest reflection.

Your ideas can be enriched, and asking your employees or associates how they would do it in your place is a good practice. The trick is never to interrupt your interlocutor. You could break off a fruitful dialogue.

Some people outside your company have an exciting activity and can help you directly or indirectly through their contacts. You know people, and they do too, so why not try to help each other? Even if their field may be far from yours, there are always good practices in other sectors that can be transposed.

Control Freak and A Judge

Both situations can be a real pain for companies. If you seek to control everything, you will spend your time behind your collaborators, who may feel it as real pressure on your part and produce less. Controlling everything is, above all, a waste of time for you, and a minimum of trust can become a real benefit because you can dedicate your time to other tasks, whether they are priority developments for your company or the fact of agreeing to a bit of rest from your already busy schedule.

Conversely, and as the saying goes, trust does not exclude control. Your role as a business manager is to make sure that everything is going well within your company.

In your management, if your conversation is mainly made up of judgments about your various collaborators, you give your interlocutor the impression that you will later judge them. Employees will be afraid to open up to you, establish dialogue, and often be forced to shut up altogether. As a manager, it remains dangerous to be dogmatic, that is, to state one's opinions as broad general principles, at the risk of appearing like a Mr. or Mrs. "I know everything." Give your opinion, but don't pretend to be right in all circumstances—the idea of your employee counts. Let them know that they will be even more valued and more productive!

Pessimistic

Adopt a positive attitude! The constantly pessimistic manager will transmit this lousy mood to their teams, and the company's activities will not turn out as well as they would like. Be careful because the economic context does not favor foolproof optimism, and you could quickly get into the bad habit of complaining regularly! Not only will you damage the morale of your teams, but you will damage the company's image through this lack of enthusiasm.

On the contrary, most managers must be great optimists who have already launched themselves into creation, have complete confidence in themselves, and never let the negative side take over. Tell yourself that moping is one of the best ways to fail.

Lack of Integrity and Stubbornness

Trust is the cornerstone of teamwork, and teamwork is the cornerstone of organizational performance. People trust you when you do exactly what you say. Trust from your subordinates is a prerequisite for successful company management.

You lack honesty if you do not tell the truth, including making inflated promises that you cannot keep.

The unrealistic fear here is that your truth is not "good" enough, and you are afraid that people will reject it, including you.

Integrity is an essential attribute of a strong leader. But do not confuse it with stubbornness. A stubborn manager does not leave others a choice: it will be the way I want it or nothing. Such behavior can provoke manipulation on the part of employees.

Bullying

Over the people who are engaged in bullying, someone was also mocked. Someone taught them that human interaction is about dominating and winning everything. They are afraid of being on the losing side.

Considering that the first prerequisite for leadership success is that subordinates need to feel you care, intimidation will not work in your favor. People can tell if a hooligan leads a group if the local order is that "beatings" will go on until morale improves.

The unrealistic fear here is that the manager is not confident enough to participate in an equal, mutually beneficial relationship. They are forced to crush other people with their power to hide their fear.

Impulsiveness

Throughout the day, we feel emotional impulses. Wise and mature people analyze these urges before giving in to them.

One successful manager said, "You don't care about your employee unless you ever think about strangling him with your bare hands." That being said, you probably don't want to indulge this temporary impulse towards someone you care about.

Maturity and wisdom are the results of the excellent integration of your thoughts and feelings over time ("What happens after I do this? How will it affect the people I care about?"). Without this integration, you get Ready, Aim, Fire! You act quickly and make decisions that could significantly impact you as a manager and the whole company.

The unrealistic fear here is that if you don't express your feelings right now, you won't be able to express them at all.

An idea comes to mind. The habit of making decisions on the go. The pattern of excessive vigorous activity for no reason. These managers don't do any research before acting on all the ideas that come to them.

All this is great! But between the idea and the call-in management are functions such as planning and organization. Planning includes risk analysis and risk management.

Of course, after a few days, or even hours, when the tasks have already been assigned, and the employees have begun to complete them, the manager understands that they hastened! The idea is not productive and poorly thought out.

The manager cancels the task.

How do employees look in such a situation? Like fools, really. Motivation is destroyed. Especially if the employees did too much preparatory work, putting aside other essential things for the sake of this goal, they are frustrated.

But I agree with the manager! Sometimes a decision needs to be abandoned. These are the realities of business—the habit of not thinking through decisions before making them.

It quickly becomes a habit to do this all the time: make a decision, then cancel it. Make a decision, then cancel it.

Liberal managers are incredibly guilty of this. They build human contact with people and then business. They don't have to change their minds! After all, they are simply sure that the employee will "understand everything"! The employee is a "good person"! And what is there to discuss? "Life is life."

The manager expects employees to understand.

One lousy manager habit leads to another bad habit for the employee-to do nothing until they are reminded a hundred times.

Employees can no longer start quests without being repeatedly kicked. They are waiting. Suddenly, the leader, "as then," will cancel the task, and nothing will have to be done?

This is an even worse habit! After all, you teach the staff to violate your orders, not to do what you order. If the inactivity lasts for a long time and you forget to check, there simply won't be enough time for execution.

Executive discipline is thus destroyed in the company.

Talkativeness

The next bad habit is that, after setting the task, the leader does not immediately release the employees from themselves but, being prone to sociability or moralizing, "chatters" the question. They share an incredible amount of detail, assessments, and conflicting opinions.

They spice up their story with a story from life. They share their experience and ask questions about other topics. Oddly enough, this happens even with a small work organization for an employee. Some managers enter multi-line comments on a task into a computer program. And they make incredibly detailed checklists in automatic control programs.

As a result, the employee can't set the primary goal of the job for themselves. Their attention wanders. They are not focused on the essentials. People who talk a lot when they put on a task almost always don't do well. This is true both verbally and in writing (in your office's computer program).

Endless discussions of various sides of this issue. Unnecessary business meetings on occasions that do not require the general presence.

In many companies, line managers listen to overly talkative top managers for hours at meetings, barely hiding their irritation and fatigue. But then they also hold seminars that never end on time in their work teams.

As a result, an eight-hour working day is not enough for people to cope with the entire volume of tasks.

And at the end of the month, companies discover that their business plans have not been met.

Trapped in An Efficiency Mindset

The habit of looking for the guilty among employees, transferring responsibility from oneself to employees in cases where things do not go as planned,

Blaming staff for failures is a bad habit of a manager. It destroys the boss's personality and negatively affects the team spirit.

Why Does This Habit Destroy the Leader's Personality?

Our task is to become an ideal manager. This means being able to manage under conditions of limited resources. If you refuse this, you will become accustomed to irresponsibility. It weans us from one another, but it's already a good habit-efficiency no matter what. If the habit of blaming the staff is not fought, the manager becomes a person who finds a thousand external reasons for their low efficiency over time.

Personnel is a very "limited" resource. The manager does not manage the entire personality of the employee but only the part that is involved in the work.

Here, a machine tool, unlike an HR resource, is at the complete disposal of the manager. A man is an emotional being. The leader achieves results through influential thinking and emotions. We can only hope that the worker puts their mind into the process. But many works automatically, without thought.

Automatic movements in some business processes are sound. They save time. They replace the need for employees to think about the details. Imagine! Why put ice cream in boxes on the conveyor, thinking deeply about the action? The machine thought of everything for the man. The work requires mechanical movements.

Office work can require thoughtfulness. The manager will be lucky if they inspire the employee to solve the problem seriously. They do the job not mechanically or formally, being distracted by phone calls, communication with colleagues, and other important work.

I use a computer to look up employees' professional skills. Often, the computer says that this person isn't fully involved in the work and is only occasionally excited about the process.

The manager fights with the employee for their inclusion, attentiveness, concentration, motivation, and responsible approach—for displaying a high level of awareness in the performance of a task.

Our task is, where necessary, to get the employee involved in the process. People are not lazy; they don't want to think. Where does this desire come from if "everyone will blame you anyway" in case of failure?

There is no comprehensive analysis of failures. Employees see that the manager does not think about anything either. And the judgment is made immediately.

Consequences of the habit: the leader is dissatisfied with the staff's "hard work." For employees: even more demotivation. even more formal approach to the performance of duties. "If only there were no complaints," the worker thinks, doing everything for this and not a drop more than the norm.

With such a habit, you will have to forget about exceeding the standards set for feats, quality, and diligence.

"The manager scolded because they're the boss!" the employee concludes after the next dressing of the head. And they don't care about the criticism at all.

The habit of blaming staff for failures forms a familiar pattern: the employee gets used to the fact that they're "always to blame" no matter what they do, no matter how hard they try. Hence, "Why should I even try then if I'm guilty anyway?"

"NO" Culture

You first say "no" and only then begin to comprehend the request or proposal that has arrived. Familiar? Such a habit sets the stage, not for a constructive dialogue in the "win-win" mode but confrontation. By denying a request in response to a request, you provoke an employee to go on the defensive: to insist, justify, reproach. This does not promote mutual understanding, trust, and cooperation.

Procrastination

A bad habit, or a story about how one businessman procrastinated, procrastinated but did not procrastinate. And rightly so: if you continue to put things off until later, their number will grow like a snowball, and with the problems come checks, fines, and other unpleasant things. Delaying the implementation of ideas is also not good.

Firstly, they may come to mind as your competitors, who will be the first to take off all the cream. Secondly, the longer you put it off, the less likely the idea will be brought to life. And it's better to do it and regret it than not to do it and bite your elbows.

You may have trivialized the adventure over the years of running the company, or you may simply need to take a breather. You have gotten into the nasty habit of putting off until tomorrow what you could do today. And yet, procrastination is the classic vice of business managers.

But why are specific tasks postponed? Already, and it must be admitted, we tend to defer particular missions that we do not like or want the least to carry out. That's why it can be so easy to become a champion of the ostrich technique, which is when you don't do anything that makes you feel stressed or tired.

Two immediate solutions are available to you to avoid carrying out all these missions that you did not do in a hurry and to take the risk of ruining them. First, place them at the top of your to-do list (and therefore execute them first) to avoid constantly postponing them; second, delegate. Nothing could be simpler: write a list of those you hate more than the others and train a collaborator who, on the contrary, likes this type of task. If you do not have enough internal resources, hire a service provider who can carry them out. So, you can focus on your core business and what you love.

Comparison

Wow, this is a deadly path. Constantly comparing yourself and your successes with the lives of other managers, you seem to evaluate yourself and often, alas, lose. Stop! The school has long since ended; there are no more losers or excellent students! There will always be someone better and more successful than you. In addition, such thoughts throw you back several steps.

Until recently, you seemed to yourself intelligent and successful, able to create and develop your own business, but now it turns out that the neighbor's garden has greener grass and more customers. This reduces motivation, causes a feeling of envy, and significantly impairs motivation, driving into depression and stress.

Gender Stereotypes

We know it well: received ideas are hard to fight. And when it comes to inequalities between men and women, they are remarkably tenacious. A new study focusing on gender stereotypes in the business world again supports this observation. Men are better at action, negotiation, and leadership, while women have a better eye for detail, listen better, and have more empathy.

Managers who think this way are more likely to believe that women aren't good managers when they work in jobs that don't match their gender.

Toxic Influences on Organizational Culture

Negativity can show up and change an organization's culture if it doesn't have the right direction and positive people around it.

It has been found that organizations where the culture is really in line with the organization's vision and strategy are more successful. But this is not always the case. Only a tiny percentage of employees believe their company effectively stewards their desired culture. Furthermore, another 5% assume that their company lacks a strong work culture. What could be causing this? So, it's good to check the culture within your organization.

Bad Communication

Companies must ensure that managers effectively and regularly communicate values, vision, standards, goals, and significant changes. This allows employees to understand the processes that take place fully. If there is little bottom-up communication, employees will not feel heard. Or they feel too intimidated to say anything, encouraging fear rather than respect.

People will never be happy when jobs are cut, but taking the time to explain the reasons for downsizing shifts the mood from wanting to leave the ship to mutual understanding.

Toxic Workers

Too much competition and a lousy work environment lead to less knowledge sharing, more corporate politics, and the spread of destructive norms.

Employees exposed to a toxic work environment or toxic co-workers are more likely to be fired for misconduct, spreading toxic behavior within the organization. This is magnified when the individual is in a position of authority, causing a snowball effect from managers to employees. In other words, say goodbye to "toxic" employees.

Resistance to Change

Phrases like "we always do things this way," "that won't work here," and "it's not my problem" hinder progress. A Google investigation into collaboration revealed the following: In 258 companies, 73 percent of employees believed that their company could be more successful.

The foremost improvement opportunity is more flexible collaboration. But the most significant barriers to creating a culture of the partnership were:

- Changing work styles and habits.
- A lack of incentives to collaborate
- Lack of leadership

Hyper Competition

Of course, it's OK if employees feel that they have to meet specific standards, but things can go wrong quickly. Within many organizations (especially in banking and other corporate solid cultures), we see that a kind of hyper-competition is slowly emerging.

Few things affect organizational culture as much as unhealthy competition. Competition can cause a split in the workplace, leading to more gossip, politics, and the courage to speak up for what you believe in.

Micro-Management

When people are constantly scrutinized, an atmosphere full of tension can develop. Close your eyes and just think of cooking a meal while two people are looking over your shoulder and a third is standing by with a fire extinguisher.

Nice feeling? We already thought

Even though micro-management doesn't work, it will lead to delays and unnecessary pressure on employees.

Do you want to prevent this? Avoid micro-management. Trust your recruiting process and trust your employees. Creating an excellent corporate culture is easiest when tasks are straightforward and, simultaneously, the individual can work autonomously and at a comfortable speed.

Bad Habits

Bad habits often start at the top of the organization. If a company's management has terrible habits when it comes to working, they can easily pass them on to employees believing that this is the right way to do business. For example, if a manager is always late, employees will learn that this is okay. Ultimately, this will create an incredibly damaging corporate culture.

Office Gossip

Gossiping is harmful no matter what environment one is in. Office gossip can be painful and hateful. This can be detrimental to the atmosphere in the office, changing the culture and even making bullying normal.

To deal with this, it is best to speak directly with those in the office who are the subject of gossip and those spreading it. After this, it is best to address the entire group that the story has infected immediately. As a side note, gossip is often linked to the bad behavior of "toxic" employees, which we talked about earlier.

Lack of Empathy

When it comes to human interaction, empathy is essential. But if employees experience too little heart, they will soon no longer feel involved in the organization. After all, everyone, including the sheepdog manager, wants to feel heard and understood. Engaging employees and having empathy for them and their lives is essential to having good relationships and strong work culture.

The Escape Plan

Good managers have strong organizational skills. Good managers have solid decision-making skills. Good managers do essential things.

Exceptional managers do all of the above and more. Of course, they care about their company and the customers and their employees and suppliers.

Most importantly, they care exceptionally about the people who work for them.

And because of that, extraordinary managers give every employee:

1. Autonomy and independence

Great organizations are built on optimizing processes and procedures. Nonetheless, each task has a best practice manual or is managed micro-level.

Engagement and satisfaction are primarily based on autonomy and independence.

Furthermore, freedom fuels innovation; even vigorously process-oriented positions have room for different approaches.

Whenever possible, give your employees the autonomy and independence to work the way they work best. Find ways to do your job better than you thought possible when you do it.

2. Zero expectations

While every job must include a certain degree of independence, it also needs to meet basic expectations.

Criticizing an employee who gave a discount to a customer who was angry today, when it was common to do so in the past, makes your employee's job impossible.

Few things are more stressful than discovering that the game's rules have changed overnight.

When a great manager changes a standard or guideline, you need to tell everyone right away.

3. Significant goals

Almost everyone is competitive; often, the best employees are highly competitive, especially themselves.

Meaningful goals can create a sense of purpose and add meaning to repetitive tasks.

Also, goals are essential. With no objective to achieve, work ends up becoming just an effort.

And no one likes wasted effort.

Offer significant challenges to your employees.

4. A sense of purpose

Everyone likes to feel part of something bigger. Everyone wants to feel that team spirit that turns people into real teams.

The best missions involve having a tangible impact on the lives of the customers you serve. Let employees know what you want to achieve in your business, for your customers, and even in your community.

5. An opportunity to provide meaningful information

The employees involved have ideas. Taking away their chance to make suggestions or quickly dismissing your ideas causes them to go astray right away.

That's why exceptional managers make it incredibly easy for their employees to make suggestions. They ask for it.

They help employees feel comfortable by proposing new ways of doing things. When an idea isn't viable, they always have enough time to ask why it isn't feasible.

6. A true sense of connection

Every employee works for a salary, but all employees want to work for more than one salary: they want to work with, and for people, they respect and admire.

It's for this reason, a friendly word, a quick casual conversation about family, or to see if an employee needs help.

These moments are much more important than group meetings or formal evaluations.

A true sense of personal connection is needed. That's why exceptional managers show that they appreciate people, not just the employees.

7. Be consistent.

Most people don't mind a strict, demanding manager with astute feedback if they treat everyone equally.

Exceptional managers know that the key to consistency is communication: the more employees there are to understand decisions, the less likely people are to assume favoritism.

8. Private reviews

No employee is perfect. Every employee needs constructive feedback. Good managers give this feedback.

Great managers always do this alone.

Don't humiliate your employees in public. Always criticize individually.

9. Public exaltation

Every employee has something exceptional. Every employee deserves their share of praise and thanks.

It's easy to recognize some of your best employees because they always do extraordinary things.

You may even have to work hard to find reasons to recognize an employee who simply meets the standards, but that's part of it.

A few words of praise, especially public recognition, can be the thing that makes an average employee into a great artist.

10. The chance for a great future

Every job must have the potential to lead to more incredible things. Exceptional managers invest time in developing employees for the work that will be great in the future.

How can you know an employee's dream? Ask!

Employees only care about your business after you've first shown that you care about them.

One of the best ways is to show that while you certainly have hope for your company's future, you also have hope for the end of your employees.

The Habits of Highly Successful Managers

Success is a daily routine, a daily commitment that works around your life's purpose. Highly successful managers understand that success in any form is not an event; it's a process. The most outstanding managers understand that success is cultivated over time.

To stand out as a manager, you must create habits that support your success and your good reputation. Once these habits become part of your daily routine, you set yourself up to become the great leader of your success and help others achieve theirs.

The difference between a good manager and a great manager is the habits they master. Here are some behaviors you can develop to become a better manager:

1. Read every day.

Successful managers know and trust the undeniable benefits that the habit of daily reading offers them. Reading will make you smarter and better at everything you do in the long run. It will make you smarter because it makes you smarter. It will make you smarter because it makes you smarter.

Reading is an activity that relaxes and stimulates you at the same time. To be a great manager, you must always be willing to step through the learning door. The learning you gain from reading dramatically increases your potential for success.

2. Focus on challenging tasks.

Exceptional managers live and thrive in the arena of challenge. The more you challenge yourself to succeed, the greater your confidence in your ability to do it again. A challenge not only helps to increase your skills and knowledge, but it also helps to increase the belief you have in yourself that you can achieve the goals you set out to achieve.

Seasoned managers are clear that there's a difference between taking on a challenge that allows them to flex their muscles and increase their skills and one that's simply a recipe for disaster. However, while navigating on autopilot, you cannot improve your skills. To become a great manager, you must get in the habit of focusing on high-level tasks that will take you and your team to the next level.

3. Learn from people you admire.

Exceptional managers tend to be more enterprising and are often overly critical when making mistakes. To avoid getting caught in this trap, successful managers make sure they have superiors or others they admire to consult with when necessary.

Experienced managers deeply understand and respect the concept that all leaders need leaders. When you have someone to look up to, it helps alleviate the acute panic you naturally experience when under the stress of challenging circumstances. Getting advice from someone you admire helps return you to an emotional state of composure, which allows you to navigate the stressful obstacles you are facing more successfully.

4. Plan your next day the night before.

The critical success habit of an effective manager is to plan the next day the night before. How can you succeed if you are unclear about what you plan to achieve on any given day? You may have certain things accomplished, but you will not be organized, and you may find yourself mistakenly focusing on tasks or details that make no difference to your big picture. Planning your next day—the day before—prepares you to start your day in an organized flow, allowing you to get more done in less time.

5. Keep your goals in front of you.

Making it a habit to have your goals before you is invaluable to increasing your success. Many managers teach the art of writing goals and then rewriting them every day. Others say it's good enough to read plans aloud once a day.

The basic idea is to keep goals fresh in your mind to ensure that you are on track to achieve them. If you don't employ this practice, it's straightforward to lose sight of what you're looking for. Instead of leading your life, you realize you're just reacting to what comes next. By having the habit of meditating on your goals, you work towards them and achieve them more easily. Accomplishing goals in this way is fantastic; it makes success enjoyable and motivates you to keep thriving.

6. Take controlled risks.

They understand the difference between a safe bet and a bold bet. They don't take reckless risks, but they don't mind taking calculated risks—and they spend a lot of time weighing the risks and benefits before making a big decision.

As Dale Carnegie well observed, "Try your luck! Life is made of opportunities. "The man who goes the furthest is almost always the one who dares to take a risk."

A great manager is also a risk-taker. They carry out actions that can generate positive and negative impacts, and with each attempt, they try to learn a little more to improve the positive effects and reduce the negative ones.

A brilliant decision-making culture leads to steady growth, better results, and trust.

7. Leverage knowledge within your teams.

They know the reason they've been put in charge is to get the most out of their team's resources. So, when it comes to deciding strategies or solving problems, they look to identify the best resources available to develop a solution quickly. They know that being a leader isn't about giving everyone all the answers. It's about making sure the best answer is found and used.

8. Respond instead of reacting.

Great managers have great emotional intelligence and understand that emotional responses, instinctive reactions, do not lead to the best results. They control their emotions, consider all the information, and make the right decisions, the best decisions, not just emotional ones.

9. Understand that actions speak louder than words.

If you want to know what someone believes, don't listen to what they say; watch what they do. Leadership defines a culture, but it does so by setting an example and living the desired culture daily, not just posting a vision and values on the company website. An image spoken but not lived is a vision that quickly dies.

10. Focus on finding solutions, not looking for someone to blame.

Dale Carnegie said, "Here is human nature at work: the person who did something to blame everyone but himself."

The difference is that great managers fight this trend. They know that blame is never the solution to an operational problem, a customer concern, or any other problem that arises in the business. Blame is a diversionary tactic that erodes the effectiveness and efficiency of teams. Most customers don't care who's at fault; they just want to solve the problem! Good managers need to solve problems first before looking for the root cause. This will help avoid a repeat.

11. Hire the best people available.

Leadership isn't about being the best person on the team; it's about hiring the best people, assembling the best team, and delivering the best results.

Great managers know this and have the confidence to hire people who are more experienced and skilled than they are. They don't feel the need to be the best at everything. We know that the team manager is usually one of the most knowledgeable about several topics, but if they are the only one who knows and masters everything, the team is in trouble. So, as a manager, hire the most competent people who will always add.

12. Focus on sustainable success.

Great managers leave a legacy of continued success even after they leave. That doesn't mean they avoid quick wins. No, they understand the benefits they can have in building momentum. They know that the best success is a long-term, sustainable success, which requires team buy-in and can also take time and effort to achieve, but it's worth it in the long run.

13. Understand the power of recognition.

What is recognized is repeated, and great managers understand this and seek to build a culture of recognition. They know it starts with them, and they take the time to send personal notes, offer words of encouragement, and praise people in public. The more we praise, the better the team we create.

If you want to be a great manager, the more you can adopt these habits and work them into your leadership DNA, the better the results will be.

PART 3
SOLUTIONS

ECCO

My-mindguide.com

Chapter 8

MANAGING IN TOUGH TIMES

2020 brought us a new challenge. An event that no manager was expecting. We had to speed up processes and methodologies, break paradigms, and change many business models, so we changed many of them.

But this pandemic also demonstrated the solidarity of companies and civil society. In an adverse context, they could react, readjust, and find ways to contribute to the fight against spreading the virus.

Events like this allow us to stop, take stock, and reinvent ourselves, not just as individuals but essentially as a society. This moment will demonstrate the resilience and sense of mission of great managers. It will take courage to make decisions that allow progress.

So as a manager, I know that leaders must keep in mind an essential rule of leadership. Their teams' work makes them work well, so managers need to build a trusting environment that encourages cooperation, critical thinking, and confidence.

To lead is to lead people into the future.

Hope Is Not A Strategy

Hope can give you a positive view of the future. But for your career or business, the only hope is worth little. Hope is not a strategy. So set a goal for tomorrow, next week, and next year. Focus on your destination and take action. Only then can you create opportunities and achieve what you hope for.

The future requires a different, creative way of looking at things. "Thinking differently." But not every manager or CEO dares to do this, while it can be the "savior" and turn-around of your company.

Many companies live in fear and resort to a "survival strategy" of cost reduction and reorganization rather than looking at growth opportunities.

Hoping for better times is not a strategy. Who dares to stand alongside big dissenters like Steve Jobs, Elon Musk, and Richard Branson, the men behind Airbnb and taxi company Uber, and see hope as the status quo?

Dare to Think About Your Company

Look at the success stories of recent years. Some of the most famous founders of "thinking differently" are Steve Jobs and Jonathan Ive of Apple. These are easy examples, of course.

Look at Elon Musk's entrepreneurial career. He single-handedly revolutionized many industries with his accumulated capital. He builds rockets that fly to the ISS through SpaceX and eventually takes 80,000 people to Mars. The electric car became popular through Tesla. Internet payments became easy through his PayPal.

Musk recently added solar energy by becoming chairman of the major US solar project SolarCity. And he says he doesn't do all this for the money; every dollar of profit disappears again into a project that should eventually "solve important problems for humanity," as Musk himself said.

These companies arose from a problem that had to be solved, with the vision that everything was possible. The solution came by "thinking differently" and looking differently at current business models.

Through the ages, every tidal wave of growth has been underpinned by "creativity" and "thinking differently." Look at the industrial revolution (from manual to machine manufacturing), the technological revolution (electricity and mass production, the emergence of the value chain), the digital revolution (internet), and the social revolution (social media). Now we must enter the creative process.

The Road to The Ideal Business Model
Therefore, it is necessary to take a good, critical look at your business model. Where do we want to be in two years? What do we now earn our money with, and can we keep it? Are we being overrun by competitors in the same category? Why can't we be number one? How do we make a difference so that we are always one step ahead of our competition?

The challenge is to consider each component in your business model (or your company's entire industry) as a potential candidate for innovation and market reinvention. Each piece can hold the key to renewed growth and success.

Never Waste A Good Crisis

This pandemic crisis came to demystify the figure of the omnipresent manager. However, it also came to demonstrate the need for human beings to have a constitution that conveys tranquility while clarifying the avalanche of information that reaches them. Today, it is clear that proximity isn't about being in the same place as your coworkers. It's about reinforcing the aggregating and eternal part of the company's values.

Leaders must follow a fundamental rule of leadership: the work of the people they lead is the essential thing that makes teams work.

There will always be crises in business and management life. What makes good managers better than bad ones is not their ability to avoid problems but their ability to face them with vigor, courage, and a desire to learn.

Change, which itself generates discomfort and anxiety, and the face of reality are often uncomfortable and impede progress. It doesn't seem plausible to me to continue everything the same after we overcome this virus, so it's essential to understand that there will be a new "normal" and how that will impact organizations at various levels.

Usually, amid a crisis, business managers assume that once the problem is gone, everything will return to normal—and the successful course of the past will be resumed. However, they ignore that market conditions have changed, that customers have developed new purchase options, that competitors have changed their behavior and strategies, and that the authorities' actions have been redone. In contrast, other companies take a proactive stance and prepare to build a new future during the crisis.

It will take courage to make decisions that allow progress.

Crises, failures, and problems are an integral part of the lives of organizations and businesses. Globalization, global communication networks, and the integration of production chains have created interconnected systems that circulate threats and opportunities. It is up to managers to face these realities with tenacity and courage, assuming what many people expect of them: to lead.

Avoid Snake Oil

Managers face many challenges. Some of them weigh more than others on the morale of managers. Many companies have been impacted by both the strikes and the demonstrations. But since certain suppliers' confinement and complete shutdown, managers have faced storms that have undermined their growth. But these were added obstacles that sometimes forced them to change their strategy.

A short tour of the situation makes running a business a real obstacle course.

Disputes with Partners

The first difficulty can come from within. One of the first causes of the closure of a company lies in the conflict of associates. It can have many origins: strategic divergences, poor distribution of roles between the partners, disputes related to investment, lack of skills, absence of agreement on the shareholders' pact. The situations are not alike and can lead to the associated row.

They significantly affect managers because the cause is inside them, not outside them.

The Lack of Sales

Your idea may be great; you may work as hard as you can every day and be as cheerful as possible, and yet your sales aren't taking off. This is one of the leading causes of stress for managers. It is mainly present in trades such as catering, where overnight, your establishment can fill up or empty for no apparent reason. In this kind of situation, we must not forget that you can have the best product in the world. That doesn't mean it will sell itself, evidenced by the many failures caused by not selling its product.

The Lack of Cash

We could forget it because it is a frequent situation for managers. Moreover, the lack of money in the company's coffers often leads business managers to have to "tweak." Supplier payment terms may not be met, negotiations with other institutions may be made to delay payments, and there may not be any new employees hired to grow the company.

To avoid this difficulty, anticipate as much as possible and create a comfortable "mattress" if possible by taking advantage of numerous funding opportunities. In this unprecedented context, the government has offered to postpone the deadlines. Being well informed is the key.

A Customer's Non-Payment

This is one of the biggest challenges a business can face. A dissatisfied customer who did not get what they wanted from your service can lead to catastrophic consequences for a company. Failure to pay by a customer (especially one of your main customers) can quickly lead you into a downward spiral and towards bankruptcy. To do this, anticipate diversifying your activities or your customers by not putting too much weight on your business with a single customer. It is often advised that this does not represent more than 30% of your sales.

Dismissal of An Employee

The situation is tough on the employee's side, but it is also tough on the manager's side. This situation generally involves mixing the human and the professional because it is often difficult to dismiss a person you like. Lack of skills, economic difficulties, unsuitability for the job, lack of performance, etc., can quickly lead you to separate from an employee. The most challenging thing is understanding that this situation is difficult for you and your employee.

The Closing of The Company

How not talk about it? The various redundancies, the suppliers or the employees that you will not be able to pay, the loss of your job, and the feeling of failure, the closing of a company is one of the most challenging moments for managers. For this situation to be as difficult as possible, anticipate it as soon as possible and do not go into over-indebtedness because you could have trouble getting up.

It's important to note that this is not an all-inclusive list of the managers' problems. However, the experience is often worth it because it's excellent.

Business Strategy Analysis

I was asked to analyze the business strategy somehow. They gave me a document saying it was a business development strategy. After looking at it, I saw that there was no strategy, at least not in the classical sense of what it is. I was given the usual progress report and some fantasies about how nice it would be to have something in the future.

I see similar "strategies" often. Many people sincerely believe they have prepared a business strategy for similar documents. Many people can't be wrong, so I decided to figure out what's wrong. As a result, I concluded that they showed me a strategy, not for business development, but for "retention in the chair."

Its managers have replaced the business development strategy with their retention strategy in the "armchair." Whether they did it consciously or subconsciously, it's hard to say. But, in their "strategy," there are almost no words on developing a business and making it more profitable. But there is a lot in it that exposes the strategists as the right people for the company.

Why Perform a Business Strategy Analysis?
A business strategy is a powerful tool that is a "map of business development." It indicates a clear path from point "A," where the business is now, to point "B," where the company should be after some time. Also, the strategy is a tool of motivation, acting as a "magic pendant," which does not allow you to relax.

The analysis process determines how correctly the route from point "A" to point "B" is chosen.

Analyzing a business strategy is an important event and one of the crucial stages. It allows you to exclude the "human factor" from the system and increase effectiveness. The analysis process determines how correctly the route from point "A" to point "B" is chosen, whether it is optimal, and whether the company can afford it.

The strategy does not involve self-expression. It is based on an exact algorithm, which must be adhered to 100%. If the algorithm is not followed, the output is anything but a strategy. It is essential to look at this strategy because, in 95% of cases, it includes "author's self-expression," which can't be left out. This is why its analysis is essential.

How is A Business Strategy Analysis Done?
The strategy begins with a vision, an image of the future, and business opportunities. The clearer the picture and the clearer the idea of the end, the better the resulting strategy. It is essential to conduct a thorough analysis of the invention to determine how much reality is in it and how many "wants" and "fantasies" the managers have.

Based on the vision, an action plan is developed to realize the emerging opportunities based on the available resources and worthwhile goals and the state of the economy, the market, and competitors' activity. Moreover, a plan is being prepared on how to get into the future, not for the individual author of the strategy, but the company or organization as a whole.

A real business strategy is a document that clearly describes developing a business, earning money, and getting the desired result.

The business strategy analysis showed a vision but a different personal plan. Its essence is that the manager looked into the future and saw that they were threatened with dismissal. They didn't want to be left without a job and bear responsibility, so they gave birth to a kind of "business strategy," but just a self-presentation about what a wonderful person they were.

A real business strategy is a document that clearly describes developing a business, earning money, and getting the desired result. In other words, the "strategy" I was given is a fake one. It covers the "fifth point" of the manager and shows that the company will not only not grow but also close down without it.

Who Conducts the Business Strategy Analysis?

An actual strategy gives the company hope for the future and money; a pseudo-strategy provides hope for the future and money to the "strategist." If the manager does not want someone to earn money at their expense, they must contact a specialist to analyze the business strategy. A qualified and impartial expert must carry it out.

Only an expert can remove the maximum human factor from a business strategy.

Only an expert who knows precisely what a business strategy is and its development can qualitatively assess it. Only an expert will evaluate the system up and down, analyze each letter and comma, and give it a cumulative assessment. Only an expert can remove the maximum human factor from a business strategy.

Business strategy analysis is an investment of time and money. However, the pseudo-strategy inflicts losses that are usually thousands and millions of times greater than the costs required to conduct the analysis. Business strategy is a bet. Whether she plays or not depends only on how good she is.

Changing the Company's Strategy

The first thing business managers and managing directors thought about with the advent of the next crisis was whether it was time for them to change something in their companies and their management. Because the problem came so quickly and was so big, it was hard for people to figure out how to move forward right away.

People often ask me: is it necessary to change the company now in this crisis? The question, of course, is strange: strangely, it is requested. The answer is obvious: you need to change yourself and your strategy right now. I always compare the company to the human body. There is a heart. This is software; it beats and pumps blood, carries useful substances; there is a brain, this is top management that makes decisions; there are hands; this is the back office; there are eyes; this is marketing; there are legs; these are sellers; they are also the tongue.

This organism lives for itself and suddenly finds out there is some incomprehensible new disease. It affects the respiratory system, and this person smokes. And then the question arises: is it necessary to quit smoking urgently to save yourself? It isn't brilliant to keep the old way of life under new circumstances.

Everyone who has gone through at least one crisis understands that they need to act very quickly and begin to change their operational activities, tactics, and strategy. Some people have not gone through a single crisis, and they are now slowing down a bit. I believe that, in these circumstances, a new strategy is needed for each of the lines of business. Any change in the external environment should entail a revision of the system.

Dream Business

First, you need to create an image of the future. This should be done by the person who formulates the company's strategic plans; as a rule, this is the business manager. They must imagine what their company should be, say, in a year. It is necessary to "dream" this image for yourself to understand what your business should become after this year. It sounds trite, but all world-famous coaches once just dreamed.

If you are a hired top manager, nothing prevents you from "dreaming" about the prototype of the department you manage. This is not business planning; this is the formation of a company's strategy, but this materialization of a big dream. A dream gives people hope; it "ignites" them. People are ready to follow their leader, especially in crisis; they need someone who knows where to go. Any leader should lead the team into the future; hope is a great guide.

The strategic meeting should be attended by the most critical management team members, people who have a lot of power, people in charge of the company's culture and technology, and people the manager wants to keep working with to make a dream come true.

In the Same Wave

The second step is the synchronization of ideas. Give the task to top management to write a free-form essay on the topic "How do I see the company's future?" The main requirement for the future is that the organization reach a qualitatively new level. This is a critical moment for a business manager: you will see how your top managers are skeptical or optimistic; you can get ideas because you do not always see everything inside the company. After receiving an essay, you need to think about how to synchronize all the pictures "drawn" by your managers with each other; for this, you need a common platform, preferably not an office, so that "the walls do not interfere."

The third step is to get together and discuss the types of future events. I did a similar strategy session at my company, but my mistake was that I brought everyone together, even newcomers. I am confident that those who have already worked for the company and are familiar with the brand will create a future prototype. First of all, these should be the team's key players; then, you will get rid of the "excessive noise."

As a result of this step, we must identify megatrends: what is happening now in the world, what can we notice to create the right image of the future of our company? Without considering megatrends, it is impossible to dream about the future. It will be just a crazy fantasy.

Megatrends of The Future

What trends can be identified?

This trend has been around for a long time. And if you didn't notice it, didn't rebuild your business for it, it's hard for you now. So far, the virus has done everything for those pulling online. Those who were not present, for whatever reason, now see the transition as an obvious necessity. Virtual reality (VR) is another trend. Many will not return from it because they will understand that it is profitable and economical.

People now value "quick" training, i.e., short training to master a particular skill quickly. Outsourcing is also a significant trend, and it will intensify.

I will single out a few more trends: "Forced whitewashing" of business: conditions are created for managers under which it is easier for them to exist in the legal and not in the "gray" zone.

Systems of total control continue to develop. We are all "under the hood" when dreaming about the future. Do not forget to take this into account. Working with "gray" money and other semi-legal schemes should be abandoned since control over the actions of managers will intensify further. The facial recognition system and its large-scale distribution worldwide are potent trends. Refusal of cash is the construction of a financial monitoring and control system.

A healthy lifestyle, ecology, and the fight against plastic in the ocean seem to some that this is far away, but these are all global trends. The same separate waste collection, global warming, all these trends are essential for the future. They will have an impact on businesses.

Building a personal brand is a powerful trend. Sometimes this tool protects, and the client must also be able to "reach out" to you. Managers need to come out of the shadows and "shake up" their brand. The generation of employees is changing; now, they need to be managed differently, dream differently, and be motivated for other reasons other than money alone.

The freedom of thought movement is a strong trend. Refusal of oil and gas: More and more people worldwide use alternative energy sources. Disintegration at the state level: the exit of the UK from the EU, China's economic dependence on the US economy, which worries European countries. Robotization is a trend that will significantly affect the labor market and service businesses. The speed and cheapness of obtaining services and products became especially pronounced during the pandemic. Refusal of expensive brands-people become more democratic; they refuse premiums in favor of democracy and simplicity. All trends need to be analyzed in terms of their impact on your company today and into the future.

Structuring Dreams

The fourth step is to dream about what your company will be like in a year, considering all the trends that affect it. Structured and specific information should already appear here. As a result, you must answer the following questions: what kind of employees will work for us in a year; who will manage; what products and services we will offer; how to build relationships with clients; what level of customer focus will we reach; what additional services we will create; and what will the control system look like? We must describe all this in as much detail as possible.

Such work in the future is very inspiring for the team. People become the authors of their lives. They create strategies for the company's development with their own hands; in this process, a close-knit group of like-minded people is formed. As a result, you should have an image of the future that inspires you.

Fifth step: In this step, we analyze the company in its current state. To prescribe a strategy, we need to understand where we are. The process is "subtracting" the present picture from the future vision. What is left is the list of active projects that need to be implemented to achieve a future prototype.

At the final stage of creating a new company development strategy, we must identify key projects that will permeate all levels of the business. In the end, everyone should find out under what slogan or motto we will live in the next year or two.

Thriving in Tough Times

It's one thing to have had a bad day, but it's another when you're going through tough times. These are the moments that form the character and show us what we are capable of.

Whether we face a personal tragedy, a financial crisis, or are hit by an uncontrollable event, these are the times in life that test our will and our spirit.

Everyone reacts differently to these situations. Some angry people feel sad about their condition or blame others.

Other people stay calm, create a plan of action to move forward, and look for a positive point to relate to in these gloomy times.

The fact is, how you react to these situations in the short term can affect your long-term success.

As George S. Patton said, "I don't measure a man's success by how high he rises, but how high he bounces when he hits bottom."

Keeping these valuable tips for dealing with difficult times in mind is essential.

So how do you deal with difficult times without descending into a total panic?

1. Be positive

You have many responsibilities, and sometimes you encounter problems. See the positive side of the situation and approach the issue constructively. Do not focus on the pain and the difficulties, but instead ask yourself what solution you will adopt.

Being positive strengthens your well-being and that of your professional entourage, who will be happy to consult you. To keep this momentum going, seek the company of positive people and cultivate positive ideas.

2. Be calm and thoughtful.

Count to 10. Try to make decisions based on facts rather than emotions.

Business managers must learn to manage their stress and balance their personal and professional lives. It doesn't mean not having compassion, but reacting to people and events in a measured way, keeping self-control, and not being too reserved or rigid.

3. Accept Help

There are beautiful people around you who can help you. Don't dismiss them, or worse, don't blame them for your problems; they are only trying to help you.

4. Learn lessons from the past

Have you ever faced a similar situation in the past? Apply what you have learned in the past to these stressful situations.

5. Seek professional advice

Identify professionals who can advise and guide you. Benefit from their knowledge, experience, and points of view. They will guide you and help you make the right decisions in difficult times.

6. Face reality

Don't run away from problems; face them! Accept the situation and face it with your pain and emotions. Accept reality as it is, not as you want it to be.

It is possible to come out of a different situation and learn something real if you face the truth.

The process of resilience involves facing the crisis, the shock, sometimes accepting it in its violence to better cope with it, expressing one's emotions, sometimes one's anger, sometimes one's distress.

7. Go ahead

Tips for thriving even in tough times: Forge ahead.

Don't waste your time and energy making excuses or blaming someone. Overcome problems, think about the future, dwell on failure, dwell on past mistakes.

Every time you make plans for your future, your past will come back to haunt you. If you ignore your past, it will come back to haunt you like a boomerang in your life. You can't move on until you've made peace with your history.

If you can take stock of your problems from yesterday, your past will no longer influence you; you will be ready to move on.

8. Make thoughtful choices

Don't look for the perfect answer. There may not be just one solution. Identify the different options and put an action plan in place. You will get more results by moving forward rather than going around in circles.

9. Prioritize

Do not treat every activity or task equally. It is essential to deal with the critical functions rather than the whole list of tasks. The importance takes precedence over urgent tasks.

Set clear goals and be determined to achieve them. Writing down a list of goals that you will revisit regularly is one of the keys to success. Having a clear and detailed plan will make it easier to achieve your goals.

10. Advance step by step

Try to solve big problems by dealing with them in stages. Deal with the items one by one and try to solve them until you find the cause of the problem.

11. Stay true to your values.

Now is not the time to compromise your integrity. Listen to your conscience. Move forward according to your convictions.

12. Be loyal

Putting the interests of others ahead of your own can develop the positive energy you need to move forward. That's why if you make a promise, keep it, both to engage your employees and retain your customers.

So, you have to be careful about what you promise. Don't engage in what you can't do or what you don't intend to do.

Once you have committed to specific goals, follow the promised timelines. Your customers or collaborators will feel respected, and you will thus increase the level of trust they place in you.

13. Relax

Life is like a marathon, not a sprint. Acting quickly will not necessarily lead to the right solutions. In the end, by doing things quickly, you will only get one result: a stressful situation.

To avoid any stress, you can bet on relaxation. This will allow you to discover solutions thoughtfully, achieve your goals, and be at your best.

14. Be a leader

Previously, managers were those who imposed their orders by force. Today, being a good manager means being exemplary. Be the first to do it right before asking others to do it.

Don't be a "do as I say and don't do as I do" thing.

15. Never give up

The greatest glory is not to fall but to get up after each fall.

16. Stay Hopeful

Even when nothing seems to be going well, we must always keep hope because tomorrow will be better.

17. Learning from your past experiences

Make sure to learn from your experiences; you might face the same problems again. Life teaches us that there are ups and downs, so make sure to reduce that slack, move on, and make sense of things.

Although difficult times can demotivate you and undermine your morale, do not despair. Stay motivated and know how to restart on more positive notes by applying our advice.

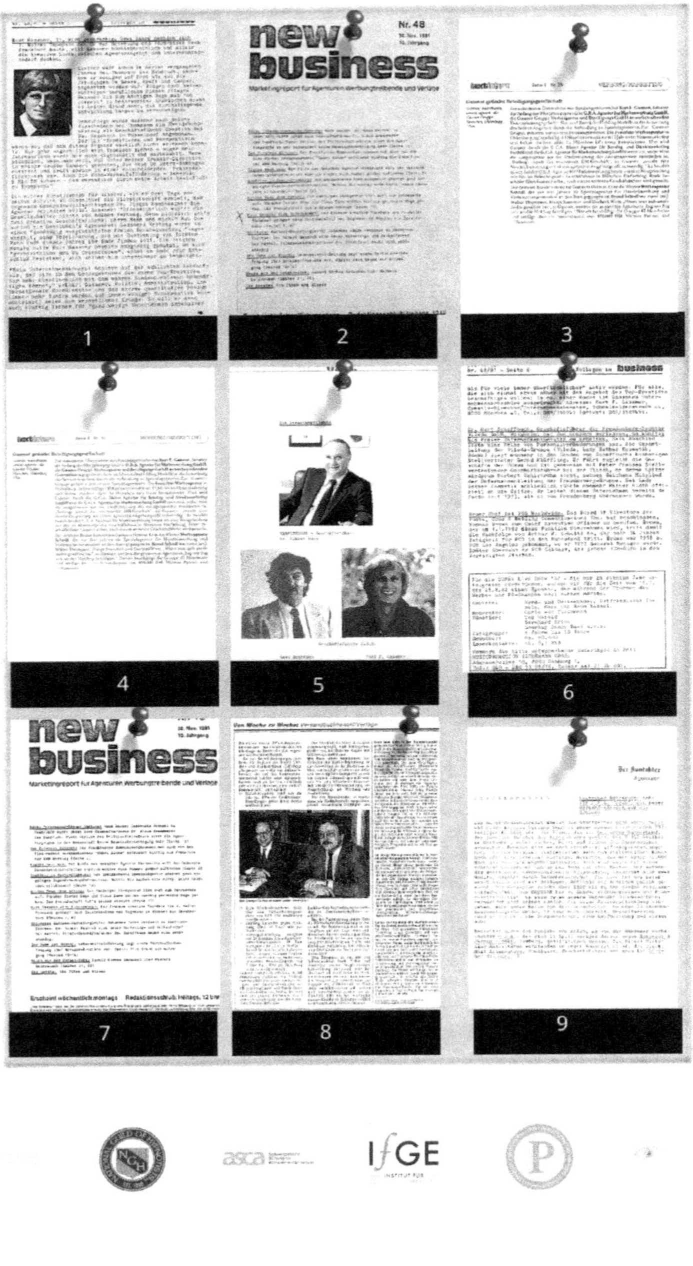

NGH

asca

IfGE
INSTITUT FÜR

P

Chapter 9

MANAGING CONFLICT

Conflict is one of the most common forms of organizational interaction and other relationships. It is estimated that battles occupy about 15% of working time. More: Managers spend even more time resolving and managing conflicts. Some organizations spend up to half of their work time on this job.

Conflicts occupy one of the central places in personnel management because of the significant time costs associated with them and the high organizational significance of their innovative, creative, and incredibly destructive consequences. At the same time, constructive conflict is the only way to find a way out of the crisis of a particular enterprise. Only its employees have information about the internal interaction and the real possibilities of the team. Conflicts are required for this potential to come to fruition in business restructuring and new ideas.

Managers do many essential things to ensure that social conflicts don't happen in the workplace. They also have to make sure that the manager does this.

A Clash of Ideas

But what is a conflict, after all? Here is an example: Suppose that two collaborators work within the same department. Mr. Legrand often works overtime. And Madame Lavender leaves precisely at 4:00 p.m. to go home. It doesn't create any conflict if the two don't find anything wrong. However, suppose Mr. Legrand wishes to return home earlier than usual. However, he can only do this if Madame Lavender stays longer in the office. In the conversation, she says, "That is impossible; I have to pick up my children at 4:15 p.m. from daycare." Until then, there is still no conflict as long as Mr. Legrand accepts this justification and puts his claims on hold.

A confrontation of interests leads to a conflict only when Mr. Legrand says to himself: "It's always me who has to back down." But my problem is that this selfish girl doesn't care at all." In this case, Mr. Legrand and Madame Lavender hinder each other in achieving their goals, which depend on each other. If Madame Lavender leaves earlier, Mr. Legrand must stay and vice versa. And because Madam Lavender refuses to stay longer, Mr. Legrand feels frustrated about his interests, which are not considered. This situation hurts him.

The three characteristics of conflict
- achieving objectives
- There is a reciprocal dependence between the participants and
- deterioration in the area of relationships.

This applies to conflicts between individual employees or groups of employees and departments or companies, for example, when they have a customer-supplier relationship.

Then, conflict resolution or management is possible. It is often necessary. Because conflicts quickly reduce performance if they are not addressed, it is required to designate someone in the company. These people have the skills to identify conflicts and deal with them quickly and provide employees with an effective tool to deal with these conflicts.

These "conflict solvers," as they are called, can be senior executives even if they cannot always manage existing conflicts. Only someone who isn't involved in the competition can deal with conflict management. This person can help the people in the conflict figure out how to find a solution or work out a deal with them if they want.

Why Conflict Management?

Conflict management is when a manager acts in the mediation of scenarios where there is a disagreement between two or more people.

Conflict, in turn, is a situation in which two parties have different interests or feelings, which can lead to confrontation or dissatisfaction on one or both sides. It is inherent in the human being, but that cannot be overlooked.

Conflicts are generally understood as a "clash of opposing elements."

However, they are more than just a disagreement; they are a deliberate act to put a stop to another party's efforts to reach its goals.

On the one hand, conflicts are necessary, and they also serve as the engine that drives change. We cannot think that conflict automatically means war or rupture; it can also be constructive.

On the other hand, depending on how they happen, they can be counterproductive and destroy value, causing damage to companies and the people who work there.

As a manager, your main job is to determine which conflicts are productive and which ones are bad for your team and how to deal with them.

Why Conflict Management?

As a leader, this is your main challenge: identifying productive conflicts from counterproductive ones and knowing how to manage them in the best way possible, turning them into positive results.

Another challenge is not using hierarchical power to resolve conflict situations in your team. As the boss, you might try to solve a disagreement by defending one person or criticizing both people.

It is inappropriate to use hierarchical power to say, "Stop the conflict because I'm in charge." This way of thinking won't get to the root of the problem, which will make things worse for everyone involved.

A good conflict manager is one who, above all, understands them. Position yourself to understand the conflict, look at both sides, be careful when taking sides, and show maturity and credibility in your decision to solve it.

How Conflicts Affect Business

When the manager doesn't get involved in the situation and doesn't try to solve problems, many things could go wrong.

Dissatisfaction: the work environment begins to get heavy, harming the emotional well-being of employees.

The decline in motivation and productivity: this dissatisfaction soon harms employee motivation and productivity.

Unresolved conflicts can lead to more people leaving the company searching for better work environments.

There is a drop in the company's competitiveness when there is a lack of communication, low morale, and talented people.

More minor conflicts are generally resolved among themselves and, in some cases, can even lead to something beautiful. For example, think of more mutual understanding or the emergence of valuable new ideas. Unfortunately, labor disputes often have unpleasant consequences for both employers and employees: a lousy atmosphere, less productivity, less job satisfaction, employees making more mistakes, and higher absenteeism. The direct result is that the workload will increase, and you will have to deal with replacement costs because of absenteeism.

The Leader's Toolkit

If your goal is to turn a particular animosity in your team into a chance to improve efficiency and results, you need to pay attention to three things.

Posture

Your posture as a manager needs to be present.

- Credibility
- Impartiality;
- Knowledge of the situation
- Loyalty and adaptability of attitudes
- The clarity in the language (assertiveness);
- Firmness in the conflict mediation process

Emotional Intelligence

The pose is important, but it's even more important if there are disagreements in your team to use emotional intelligence, especially the four most important skills:

- Self-knowledge (self-awareness);
- Self-control (self-discipline);
- Empathy
- influence (social skill).

It will be practically impossible to manage conflicts without exercising these competencies.

Leadership Styles

In addition, knowing how to manage leadership styles is a differentiator. Depending on the situation before you, think about the best leadership style you should apply:

- Coercive (requires immediate compliance);
- It is reliable (it motivates people to work toward a common goal);
- Aggregator (produces harmony and strengthens emotional bonds).
- Democratic (forges consensus through participation);
- aggressive (setting high-performance standards);
- Advisor (develops people for the future).

Sometimes it's more beneficial for you to use more than one simultaneously.

Practice Makes Perfect

It's good to know what approach to adopt when a conflict at work arises, but it's even better to have concrete examples to understand.

Of course, all conflicts are different. So, what I'm going to tell you isn't going to be a magic potion that will solve all of your problems by swiping your finger.

Instead, I will present tips and examples to help you solve them more easily.

1. Personality clashes

Some personality types can't work together, but your team members can still learn to work together without getting into fights.

The key to getting there? Be sure to encourage your team to show empathy and understanding.

When personality clashes arise in your team, encourage the people involved to put themselves in the other's shoes. Invite them to be more understanding and stop mulling over their differences.

Also, pay special attention to personality in your recruitment process. Do not be afraid to ask questions such as, "How would you react in such a situation?" Why did you leave your previous job?

Two colleagues who make the atmosphere tense

Situation

Two waitresses don't get along at all. Although they remain respectful towards each other, everyone feels tension when they are both on the floor. Clans even begin to form within your team.

How to fix the situation

As a manager, you need to meet with them to understand what's going on and help them find a solution. You can't force them to be friends, but they have to know that they need to get along in a civilized way.

Encourage them to discuss and find common ground. You can ensure that everything is done with respect by acting as a mediator.

If, despite your efforts, nothing works, you will have to find a more drastic solution. You could, for example, adapt their schedules so that they no longer have to work during the same hours.

2. Conflicts over tasks and responsibilities

Teamwork can be complex when communication isn't good because people often fight over who should do what.

Expectations or agreement.

You have probably already been told that it is essential to communicate your expectations to your employees. What if I told you it's not enough?

Instead, try to find common ground with your employees.

Rather than imposing your vision, discuss it with your team members. That way, you can agree on realistic goals.

A straightforward trick to apply daily is summarizing your remarks at the end of an exchange. Even better, ask your interlocutor to translate what they understood. This way, you make sure you are always on the same wavelength.

Involving your employees in decision-making also helps boost their commitment and motivation.

An employee who does not perform their duties as they should

Situation

Despite your repeated requests, an employee still fails to do specific tasks when closing the store. You are unhappy because you feel that they're not doing the job correctly and decide to meet and talk about it.

How to fix the situation

Start by trying to figure out why it always omits some tasks.

As you talk to them, you find that they never have time to do them. They are often busy helping customers until the last minute and can't free themselves to complete their entire to-do list.

Moreover, they can't stay long after the store closes since they must catch a bus to return home.

If you care about flawless store closing, make sure you schedule enough employees to do all the tasks.

If that's not possible, come up with a more realistic to-do list.

3. Leadership Conflicts

Leadership is a highly sought-after quality in the world of work.

However, a manager's leadership style can sometimes cause problems in an organization. This is why it's essential to make sure your team members' roles are clear and that you support your managers.

Provide training or mentoring so that your management team can healthily develop their sense of leadership. Promoting your top salesperson won't make them a good supervisor overnight.

The more tools your team has at their disposal, the more effective your management processes are.

A hostile leader in your management team

In context

You recently promoted your top salesperson to team leader. At times, they had a negative attitude and would make sarcastic jokes about the rest of the team.

In the context of a labor shortage, you could not conceive of letting go of such a high-performing employee. So, you still decided to offer them a promotion.

However, their management style is inadequate, even misplaced. Several employees even complained about how they manage the team.

How to fix the situation

Such a situation undermines a team's morale, breaks cohesion, and makes everyone feel uncomfortable. There is an excellent line between workplace harassment and this kind of disrespectful behavior.

You don't want to be the boss who lets the situation slide into a labor lawsuit.

Zero tolerance should be the watchword.

4. Conflicts in working methods

"All roads lead to Rome."

It is not because someone does not do precisely what you want that their working method is unsuitable.

It is, therefore, necessary to know how to put your ego aside. Be accommodating and open-minded.

Your employees also need to adopt the same attitude. Just because they've always done something a certain way doesn't mean you have to keep doing it.

Two employees who think their method is the best.

Situation

Two employees in your team handle orders in entirely different ways. You have no problem with their practices.

However, they are often in conflict because they say that the other is not doing their tasks properly. They clearly can't agree on the subject. It makes teamwork very difficult.

How to fix the situation

Encourage your employees to find common ground. If they can't do it on their own or feel the tension mounting, don't hesitate to have a formal meeting.

Explain to your employees that the goal is not to find a culprit or pick a winner but to find a compromise. Accompany them to find a solution that ensures that none feels injustice.

Once found, make sure the new procedure is straightforward and respected by all members of your team.

5. Serious conflicts

Any company needs to provide a healthy working environment for its employees. Even by implementing the best practices, it sometimes happens that certain types of serious conflicts arise: discrimination, harassment, intimidation, etc.

This type of conflict is very delicate to deal with, so you need professional help right away.

Ensure you have an internal policy that clearly states that these behaviors are prohibited.

Diagnosing the Debate

1. Confrontation in conflict management

Conflict Management: Containment Strategy

It involves managing the conflict through a frontal approach between the parties involved. You can sit down with the people involved on either side and propose that they each defend their position.

So, you try to learn about the positions, why they're at odds with each other and how they came to be.

In this strategy, your role is to mediate the discussion.

2. Slowing down in conflict management

Conflict Management: Deceleration Strategy
Adopting this conflict management strategy emphasizes the common interests of the people involved and minimizes the differences between the fighting people.

Try to find out how these interests can be aroused in professionals who conflict.

So, despite the differences, it is possible to show that the two parties have a lot in common and have the same goals and inclinations.

3. Collaboration in conflict management

Conflict Management-Collaboration Strategy
Propose that everyone involved put their own goals aside and work together to develop a standard plan.

This exercise allows people in conflict to think about solutions different from those proposed, a third alternative that resolves the conflict.

4. Negotiation in conflict management

Conflict Management: Negotiation Strategy
This strategy involves each party giving up something to reconcile differences.

You should talk to each side to understand where they are unwilling to compromise and be relaxed.

All sides must agree to give up some of their positions to find common ground and eliminate what is causing the conflict.

5. Behavioral changes in conflict management

Conflict Management-Behavior Change Strategy
Try to find the causes of the conflict and solve it definitively. The perspective is to change personal attitudes and behaviors.

For that, you need to discover the real cause of the conflict and act as the primary mediator.

It is also part of conflict management to define which of the two parties is right in defending their point of view.

Then, request a change in behavior from the people involved. If there is no such change in behavior, you will only be postponing this conflict and not resolving it.

Building Consensus

Conflicts in business are legion. Managers must be reactive to resolve these conflicts as quickly as possible, which is particularly detrimental to the quality of work and employees' commitment. Here are tips to ease tensions as soon as possible and limit conflict in the workplace.

Remember People Are Different
Where there are people, there will always be the possibility of conflict. I must respect the positioning of all of them. Each one has a way of perceiving the world around them, with opinions, training, and values very different from the other, so it is essential to encourage tolerance and respect among everyone.

Communicate with Your Teams
Conflict in business must be anticipated as much as possible to avoid psychological and financial costs. Defusing a conflict

naturally involves communication. Managers should talk to their teams all the time instead of waiting for the point of no return.

Get to Know Your Teams

It is challenging to communicate when you don't know your collaborators. Getting to know them means doing psychological work to find out who the driving forces are, those who seek conflict in business, etc. The goal is to treat each team member as an individual to avoid conflicts.

Improve Cohesion

Conflict in business often results from a lack of cohesion. Bringing teams together and motivating them that's the current trend. And the solutions abound. You can find out more about the benefits of team building by organizing meals with your coworkers. This gives you the chance to relax in a different setting while still bringing people together.

Respect Your Teams

Conflict in business sometimes results from tensions due to a lack of valuation. If your collaborators are efficient, and their work is high quality and delivered on time, knowing how to say it is an excellent way to motivate the troops.

Set Up A Time Management System

Conflict in business can be linked to legal and financial aspects. A simple error on a payslip, a wrong overtime calculation, and everything can change. Using a time clock, an utterly impartial tool, you will avoid many conflicts.

Play Your Role as Mediator

If the conflict involves your team members, be sure to intervene to ease the tension and ensure that the situation does not escalate. But be careful; your role as a manager is not to solve all the problems but to support the people concerned.

Encourage Dialogue Between Teams

Often, you may not be at the company when a conflict arises, so training the team to value dialogue is necessary. Identify people in the group who can act as mediators and encourage them to try to solve problems without the figure of the manager. Over time, these people will become references for the team itself.

Avoid Clashing in Conflict Situations

When there is a conflict in the company, tempers rise, people change, and everything seems more difficult to resolve. In these situations, the best thing is to avoid the clash and hold on to balance. When understanding is sought, everything becomes easier to fix, problems become more precise, and the resolution is closer. If the manager assumes a defensive posture, they contaminate the collaborators and harm the group. Dealing with these situations transparent, friendly, and open is necessary.

Use Conflict Situations to Grow

Managing conflicts within the company is an incredible opportunity to strengthen the team. The conflicting situations of everyday life should always lead the team to learn. Record these situations, with their causes and consequences, and take advantage of this material in the company's regular training sessions. The idea is that everyone realizes that, despite the initial wear and tear, the situations bring learning and growth to the group. People should not repeat the conflicts in these situations because they already have a possible way to solve them.

Bring A Solution Quickly

Conflicts have an actual cost for the company. When tensions increase, employees do not want to go to work. The manager's role is to intervene immediately to solve problems within the company. Absence due to illness or sloppy work is what these conflicts can cause.

In managing conflicts in the company's daily life, the higher objective is that the working relationship between the parties to the conflict must be restored. It is not a question of creating, from the conflict between the "leaders," a relationship in which "we love each other" or "we become the best friends in the world." The manager must act in the operating environment, which constitutes a different repertoire than the coach, for example, which is addressed to private persons. This method must be learned during appropriate training and then used professionally.

Was dem Club verlorengeht, soll eine neue Versandfirma kompensatorisch auffangen

10

Schon gelesen?

11

...Marketing

12

Der Kontakter
Anzeige der Woche

Kurt P. Gassner, Inhaber und Geschäftsführer der G.C.A. Werbeagentur in München, wählte diesmal zwei völlig unterschiedliche Anzeigen, die eines gemeinsam haben: "Sie verkaufen eine Idee." ...

13

14

Agentur GCA betreut Steinecker und DST

Klargestellt

15

Der Kontakter
Agenturen

SPEZIALISTEN

16

new business Nr. 27, Seite 16 AGENTUREN

17

Chapter 10

CREATING A GROWTH CULTURE

Strengthening the company's culture is a powerful strategy to attract and retain talent, promote a cohesive brand to the market, and, last but not least, make the work of teams more focused and enjoyable.

Organizations keep a close eye on various performance indicators every day—for example, yield, efficiency, occupancy, absence, turnover, or customer satisfaction.

Rightly so, because in today's markets, you want to be up to date as an organization and prepared for everything that might happen tomorrow.

It is of the utmost importance to have good and committed employees. They are in charge and make sure that organizations stay in business and have the right to be there.

The same employees automatically become part of the performance culture naturally.

A company does not exist without its own culture. If it were not consciously created, it would arise in the process of formation and work. The involvement of employees in the company's image depends on the corporate culture. In current market conditions, this is essential: only a client-oriented, open, and recognizable business is booming.

What is Management Culture?

It results from how people interact in an environment and how it evolves based on those interactions. When a company has a weak culture, there's no good or bad, only strong and weak. It's like a soup with 29 ingredients that taste different, but you're not quite sure why. It is the result of a great mix without consistency.

Often, the manager begins to feel pain related to organizational culture when the company grows at high speed. While growth is accelerating, concerns about sales, deliveries, and finances, for example, take precedence over conservation of culture. The need for hiring is high, and there is often no time for official training, with onboarding and immersion of new employees. The result is that we mix fresh ingredients that influence the outcome of the soup.

In essence, culture is made up of people. And when new people arrive, it is natural for them to change, evolve, or be influenced by the baggage brought by new employees from other cultures that they have lived in.

Culture is how we communicate, in all its forms, and the meaning people derive from it. From choosing the physical location, the furniture, the way the space is divided, the name, the spelling, the colors, the way we speak, the words we choose, to the tone of voice we use in each situation, We talk and decide to communicate the way we see the world, how we position ourselves within it, and what kind of people we want to relate to. And how do we expect people to respond to this?

Consciously developing a company's culture is not easy. It has to do with the consistency we generate and meeting our expectations—the examples we create, the decisions we make, and the stories we tell. And especially with the people we hire and the people we send away.

Little by little, people come to understand, mirror, and multiply what we value until it becomes second nature for the organization to be that way.

Organizational culture is more than just beer on Fridays. It defines and shapes the work environment and emerges from the set of programs, patterns of interaction, and behavior at the organizational level, not to mention business goals and values. However, building an excellent corporate culture takes time and effort.

When you work in your organization, you probably think a lot about the product you're building, how you can get customers, and the people you're hiring. Ultimately, these aspects are critical to the smooth running of the business.

It is possible to build an excellent corporate culture, but it takes a team of leaders who are actively involved in the process.

Why am I telling you all this? Because I believe that organizational culture is the key to creating an effective business, an excellent team, and, ultimately, the realization of the stated mission.

Organizational culture is at the heart of the company. It is a practical and widespread application of its norms, best practices, ideas, and shared values. Culture defines and shapes the work environment. Ultimately, the development of organizational culture is the creation of programs that help achieve business goals while maintaining a connection with the company's values.

The organization's business goals What is your organization striving for in the market, and how will it achieve this?

Corporate values: It starts with management values and a sincere commitment to these values.

People and points of interaction with them: Imagine all the policy documents, communication channels, and corporate ethics adopted in the organization. There are hundreds and thousands of issues of interaction that shape organizational culture, from the budget and the language in which job responsibilities are defined to the methods of making and communicating decisions and business goals.

Whether your company is a startup or is scaling up, looking at the culture is to ensure consistency in the organization's growth without losing sight of the values that got it where it is and will pave the way for it to take the following steps.

Why is Management Culture So Important?

Developing an organizational culture and leadership that promotes personal fulfillment, teamwork, and mutual support determines the success of your business. Corporate values are like the engine of the entire enterprise, allowing you to regularly and purposefully improve such aspects of the business as customer support, recruitment, and adaptation of new employees, internal processes, and almost everything related to the organization.

A good culture encourages employee engagement and loyalty because they feel supported and do their best every day. With a strong culture and values, you can:

- Implement team-centric workflows that enable your team to do their best work.
- Eliminate obstacles to make it easier for team members to implement high-impact projects.
- Ensure that everyone in the company is valued for who they are, no matter their gender, appearance, race, or other characteristics.
- Link everything to the organization's mission so that everyone understands why their work is so vital to the common cause.
- Set standards for teamwork, collaboration, and team building throughout the organization.

It is of the utmost importance that culture helps your employees do the most critical work most efficiently. This drives business growth, creates opportunities for our mission, and ultimately increases employee satisfaction and development.

The importance of corporate culture cannot be overstated. An influential corporate culture will allow you to create, execute, and scale successful projects and processes, increase profitability, and maintain business continuity. It will also make employees more excited about their jobs, make customers and stakeholders happy, and improve overall satisfaction.

This will establish your organization's reputation with a distinct advantage in today's highly competitive business environment. Thanks to a forward-looking corporate culture, you will be able to attract business partners, employees, or, for example, suppliers.

A solid corporate culture is most important for the younger generation just entering the workspace. While young people value a job with a stable paycheck, they also emphasize culture and emotional content to keep them motivated to work.

Cultural Variety and Differentiation

Whether you work in a small startup or a large corporation, the main goal of business is growth. Growth in the number of customers, revenue, and profit growth.

But to achieve new goals and not lose control along the way, it is necessary to form and develop a culture of growth in the company.

Often, the corporate culture comes first, including a well-equipped office, table tennis, consoles, free drinks, and other cookies.

Unfortunately, this is not a fundamental attribute of its culture and does not correlate with its growth plans. This is just a simple way to manipulate the comfort of employees.

An authentic growth culture is much more innovative and more complex. It has three key components:

- Growth systems
- Goals and ways to achieve them
- "Psychological safety"

1. Growth system

Separate growth into its discipline and set up a system where development can be worked on all the time. This way, your company will have a culture of change.

Creating a growth system should not be a sudden event. This is a gradual, evolutionary process that runs parallel to its development.

In the growth system, like in any other corporate strategy, there must be a person in charge of instilling discipline, building a team, and getting things done.

At the initial stage, such a person is called the Growth Manager. But as the company and the system grow along with it, the position of growth manager evolves into Head of Growth, Growth Director, VP of Growth, and Chief Growth Officer.

New requirements for employees' talents are needed as part of the formation of the discipline of growth.

- Focus on results
- T-shaped skills and a willingness to learn
- An understanding of Agile and Lean methodologies
- Focus on metrics and data
- A scientific approach to experiments
- Product obsession
- Focus on clients

At the same time, the essential competencies of participants in the growth system can be different: programming, analytics, design, marketing, product management, sales.

It is essential that the company recruits new people with the right talents and develops the skills of existing employees.

2. Goals and ways to achieve them

A company's culture must be closely linked to its goals and approaches to achieving said goals to prevent growth from becoming a meaningless ritual.

It doesn't matter what kind of goal-setting system you use (KPI, Smart Goals). The work to achieve goals and results must be deeply integrated into the culture of growth.

The same is true in reverse. When you use KPI to set goals in a company that doesn't have a growth culture, you risk turning your employees into a mess, which will harm the results.

To work effectively towards growth goals, you need to take a non-linear approach to prioritization. As part of this approach, the established priority estimates for each plan must be multiplied by the growth impact factor. In this way, you can highlight the most important goals for the company within the planning period.

3. Psychological safety

According to Google research, employees' psychological safety is the main component of successful teamwork.

Psychological security means that team members are not afraid to take responsibility and take risks within their goals and objectives. Working within a team, they feel more secure than working alone.

This allows you to start the process of continuous experimentation and learning in the team, which is so essential for growth.

The process in terms of psychological safety looks like this:
a lack of fear of making mistakes; a desire to share new ideas; new experiments; innovative solutions

In situations where there is no psychological security, team members are afraid of criticism and mistakes, which does not allow them to experiment and discover new original approaches to growth.

Create and maintain a comfortable, open atmosphere of mutual respect in your teams so that each member can share their ideas without fear of criticism. This is very important for developing a culture of growth.

Combining a well-functioning system, a focus on goals, and mental security will allow you to create a culture conducive to growth and be ready to scale your business.

Management Culture and Identity

Strategy and culture are two of the main levers for improving the company's performance and growth. The plan talks about goals and shaping the people around them. It is associated with planning and includes adaptive elements to respond to external changes. On the other hand, culture expresses these goals through values and beliefs and introduces group norms according to which employees perform tasks. Culture is not a strategy. It's a lever made up of unpredictable behavior, thinking, and social patterns that change all the time.

Leaders who want to build high-performing businesses may develop intelligent strategies and goals, but their plans are doomed to fail if they don't understand the power of culture.

Culture is an organization's tacit social order; it shapes long-term attitudes and behaviors; cultural norms determine what is encouraged, prohibited, accepted, or rejected within the group. We assume that culture can be controlled. The first and most crucial step managers can take is recognizing and understanding how it works. Using this framework, managers can determine the impact of culture on their business and assess its alignment with strategy. The results of more than 100 of the most common behaviors have helped us figure out what makes up culture.

Culture can release tremendous amounts of energy towards a common goal and contribute to the prosperity of an organization. It can develop flexibly and autonomously in response to changing opportunities and requirements. Strategy is usually driven by managers, while culture can combine the qualities of senior leaders with the knowledge and experience of middle-level employees.

Four Cultures: Where is Your Scaleup?
Take a good look around you, at other scale-ups, or at companies where you have worked as an employee in the past. If you were to categorize their learning culture, where are they on the following axis?

Culture of sleep, culture of inspiration, culture of anticipation, and culture of growth.

Asleep culture is a corporate culture where innovation and learning are not DNA. This could be because of the industry or simply because too much money has been made too quickly in recent years (without innovating). Or that the organization only focuses on day-to-day operations and has no time or budget for development. Growing for years without innovating carries the risk of complacency and decline. Moreover, there is another problem: it does not attract creative and innovative talent.

An inspirational culture is not static; time and budget are invested in learning. They gain ideas and knowledge and share what they have learned internally. However, this learning is mainly limited to wisdom and insight. And if there is implementation within this culture, you will see that it is fragmented. It only happens within specific roles or functional areas, such as IT or marketing. The idea is that we mainly want to be inspired and share new ideas. It would be appreciated if you came up with many new ideas in these organizations. There is no focus on the actual changes and improvements. This culture lacks, which prevents it from becoming a growth culture, an organization-wide rhythm of implementation.

In a culture of anticipation, there is time and space for inspiration and development. There is an eye for what is happening internally and externally, and the organization reflects and anticipates developments, trends, and opportunities. Learning develops problem-driven at a company, department, or individual level. At best, it is clear the possibilities and expectations concerning education. In the worst case, this is from HR, instructed that people should develop. Then supply and demand meet visibly. In practice, the learning culture relies on external stimuli and a few internal individuals who drive learning and implement it. The implementation is mainly problem-oriented and not future-oriented. The learning culture is primarily designed to keep up to date.

The best scaleups manage to find a balance between learning and implementation. They have integrated working for the company integrally into the entire organization and work from a so-called **growth culture.** The objectives follow logically from the strategy. If one of your success strategies is to build a winning international company culture, it makes sense that the entire organization learns about it and can implement it. Of course, you also have goals at the departmental and individual levels. Organizations with a growth culture often work with a 90-day or quarterly rhythm, in which each team can formulate a specific and concrete growth goal.

Managing Cultural Change

You have probably already found yourself in front of someone who said something to you but whose tone and non-verbal expression expressed the opposite. What happens in this case? You may not trust what is being said, and you will give more credit to how you feel than to official messages. It's normal; the verbal weighs only 7% of what we perceive in communication.

Well, in corporate culture, it is the same. If there is a gap between an official corporate culture (the words) and what is lived, it is always what is lived and felt that would prevail.

To avoid this gap, it is necessary to be particularly vigilant about two elements:

The role of HR and managers They are the primary vectors of the corporate culture. It can be read in what they say, especially how they make their decisions.

Consistency between values and decisions made. It's about linking what is displayed and what is done. This will avoid creating vagueness, incoherence, or even paradoxical injunctions. Knowing how to recognize decision-making in the old culture shows humility.

Today we talk more and more about cooperation, collective intelligence, empowerment, and autonomy. Many business managers want to highlight these postures in the culture of their organizations. However, some upstream work may be needed to align core beliefs and values with Indeed; a lack of harmony will harm the company's ambitions.

It is essential to distinguish a value from a belief clearly. In a simplified way, an idea makes it possible to define the true and the false, while a deal makes it possible to distinguish the good from the bad.

Let's take the concrete example of a company that wishes to develop autonomy. It, therefore, includes the latter in its values to encourage the associated behaviors. However, if the beliefs of the hierarchy imply that employees cannot be trusted, then there is a fundamental conflict between the value of the company and its ideas. This gap will show up sooner or later because our deep beliefs are reflected through our reflexes and behaviors. It will then be tough to keep the new culture and its goals in place.

The same rules apply to all managers, whose words and actions, which are more closely watched, must be in line with each other.

We are at a historical period where the beliefs "of the world before" can no longer coincide with the "world after" ambitions.

For your company to succeed in the next world, it will often be necessary to review the corporate culture, whether for a simple "refresh" or a profound transformation. It will be essential to make sure that everyone's and everyone's beliefs are in line with the common postures.

Universal Cultural Values

Everything about a growth culture is about creating an environment that encourages productivity, creativity, and sharing experiences.

For this, all managers and employees must follow some fundamental values. Check out these features below.

Safety

A common mistake many professionals make is trying to accuse someone else whenever something goes wrong. This creates insecurity as everyone feels pressured and is afraid of reprisals.

In this growth culture, all company members must be prepared to take responsibility for their failures.

This attitude must start with the managers, who serve as an example for other employees. If managers act fairly and transparently, subordinates tend to replicate this behavior. Thus, the team starts to have more autonomy and responsibility and achieve better results every day.

Continuous Learning

One of the main characteristics of the growth culture is that it encourages continuous learning.

Establish open management, with space for questions, whatever they may be. No one should be judged by a question, however obvious it may seem. Thus, everyone feels free to ask questions and improve their performance.

In addition, take care of the professional development of employees. Offer training that enhances their strengths and helps them develop new skills. In this way, everyone wins the employee, who increases their chances of growing in their career, and the company now has a more prepared team.

Innovation

Innovation is essential for a company to grow. Therefore, the search for new experiences, boldness, and courage must be part of the organization's routine.

It sounds easy in theory, but few managers can put it into practice. That's because thinking outside the box involves taking risks, and most companies are very tolerant of mistakes.

However, it is necessary to change this pattern to achieve adequate growth. Allow professionals to present and test their ideas. Give them all the support they need to develop their projects in the best possible way. Many will not bring any results, but the one that works can change its level.

Feedbacks

Feedback is one of the great pillars of the growth culture. Bear in mind that a formal and periodic performance evaluation is not enough, as is common in large companies. Feedback needs to be continuous to be effective.

Praise, give constructive criticism, and help employees evolve every day. Don't wait for a date in the year or every six months to tell employees their successes and failures. Thus, evolution becomes faster, both for professionals and for the company.

Furthermore, it is not just managers who should give feedback. Allow employees to review their leaders and peers. Everyone assumes the commitment to help develop people and the organization.

Empathy

An authentic growth culture also involves paying attention to how people feel and behave. Therefore, always consider the personal needs of employees and professional ones.

Be flexible, listen to what employees say, and try not to overwhelm the team. Leaders must always be open to dialogue and help employees with whatever they need. This makes the team more confident in the managers and feels more secure performing an excellent job.

Positive Climate

Company growth is directly related to team productivity. As we have seen throughout the article, many factors influence performance, and one of the main ones is the quality of the organizational climate.

It's not new that employees who are happy with their work environment do better and do more.

Therefore, implement actions that keep the company's climate consistently high. Promote happy hours recognition events, and encourage good relationships among all team members. This way, you guarantee good results and constant growth for the organization.

Keep in mind that performance should not be the company's only focus on a day-to-day basis, but rather the satisfaction and engagement of the team. That way, you ensure a much more efficient and lasting evolution!

The culture-shaping Toolbox

It is widespread for managers to feel that, without them, nothing happens. After all, it was the same in the beginning! But now that demand has increased, the response must be faster, and it can't be that way anymore.

How can the organization keep up with this pace without losing the unity and essence that you, as managers, fought so hard to build? Through the propagation of culture by leadership!

Strong and inspiring managers keep the company's purpose and mission in mind, knowing the why behind their work. But this also needs to be aligned with everyone in the organization.

In a way, a solid and well-aligned culture among the leadership "contaminates" the organization as a whole.

Creating A Company Growth Culture

A few years ago, our company integrated another one as an acquisition. Two flourishing organizations with an enviable situation came together: good leadership, dedicated people, and great recognition in the market. However, we underestimated certain crucial elements: the style of leadership and specific fundamental values diverged between the two organizations; two completely different cultures faced each other.

Thus, this integration, which was simple and to is accomplished in harmony, was relatively a period of conflict, leading to employee frustrations. In the wake of this adventure, we have identified the following leads that I am sharing with you to awaken your reflection on the sustainability of your culture in the context of rapid growth and your influence on it as a manager.

Are you a company manager implementing change in the workplace? We present to you the best ways to improve corporate culture.

1. Formation of common values

Forming common values and an unwavering commitment to them is the key to an excellent corporate culture. The core values of an organization reflect how team members should treat each other and how they can expect to be treated, and these are the central values shared by every employee of the company.

At the same time, it is important not to plant values but to provide colleagues with the opportunity to create cultural values themselves. Company values are the ideals your colleagues believe in and should be alive and dynamic, just like the company itself.

A value refresh is an effective way to improve, redefine, or create new value based on a company's stage of development.

Sometimes this means rethinking or updating values, especially as the company grows.

2. Promoting Diversity, Inclusion, and Inclusion

A key aspect of organizational culture is that employees feel they are an integral part of the whole. And that perception starts with diversity, inclusion, and inclusion. In addition to being just the right thing to do, building diversity in your workforce also gives you a competitive edge. Research shows that companies with a high level of diversity are more innovative, make better decisions, and achieve their financial goals more successfully.

So how do you promote diversity? There are some great ways to implement variety in a culture, for example,

- **Equal opportunities in the selection and adaptation of new employees.** To create a diverse culture, start by hiring and onboarding employees. Train hiring managers to be inclusive in the hiring process. Try to find and attract minority candidates. Focus on creating equal opportunity when working with candidates. Finally, make sure that HR and recruiting professionals always encourage diversity and inclusion during the hiring and onboarding process.

- **Employee support groups.** Employee support groups are places of protection for minorities. They form a sense of belonging to a community consisting of all their collective members. Although employee support groups are usually created at the company level, they are often run by team members willing to shape the work culture.

- **Frank communication.** To make your team feel comfortable, ensure that you can express your thoughts frankly at work.

For example, we have so-called "heart-to-heart talks" to discuss complex and even uncomfortable topics such as self-identity and problems at work. Such frank and open conversations help employees to be themselves.

- **Inclusive spaces.** Another way to ensure that employees can be themselves is to make sure that they are comfortable even just being in your company. For this purpose, mother-and-child rooms for working mothers, prayer rooms, shared toilets without gender separation, and facilities for universal accessibility are being created.

3. Cultivating mutual trust

An inclusive culture is based on trust. Employees should express themselves freely so that they are not afraid to experiment, make risky decisions, and even fail, but ultimately develop individually and in a team setting. One of the elements of building an organizational culture is creating a space in which employees, regardless of their position, position in the team, and length of service, will readily share their ideas and thoughts.

Open and honest communication among employees must be encouraged to maintain mutual trust. There are several ways to implement this condition in corporate culture:

- **Creation of places for open communication with the company's management.** One way to show colleagues that you trust them is to approach company managers with specific questions. Even if it's a meeting with the whole management team or a quick brush every month on a different topic, showing that you're willing to answer questions builds trust between you and your coworkers.

- **Feedback at all levels.** The downside of being open is accepting input from peers. Disagreement is critical to effective collaboration, and constructive criticism helps build a stronger bond with team members. Learn how to provide constructive feedback.

- **They are increasing the transparency of projects, processes, and decisions.** Whenever possible, keep information public or share essential choices through a single source. Sometimes, team members just want to understand what's going on and why a particular decision was made.

4. Allocation of responsibility as needed

At the heart of the building, trust is the opportunity for employees to participate in certain stages of the decision-making process. This can be done in many ways, but sharing responsibility works best. Instead of just cogs in a giant machine, employees should feel like meaningful partners.

When everyone in the team can reach their full potential, everyone can do much more for the company. In our experience, when an organization has the right balance of power, employees are more satisfied, and their most challenging tasks get done more quickly.

5. It increases clarity and reduces fragmentation.

Clarity is the key to an efficient work environment and, as a result, a solid corporate culture. Often, work is scattered across different groups and tools, making it difficult to access. Without a clear understanding of what needs to be done and why, it can feel like the wheels are turning, but you are not moving anywhere.

If you haven't already, provide a clear and actionable way to tie daily work toward company goals. According to a recent study, only 26% of knowledge workers have a clear idea of how their work relates to company goals. This is because setting goals in a presentation or spreadsheet that is updated quarterly does not provide enough connection to the work that is done daily.

To prevent this from happening, you can increase motivation and ensure clarity by tracking company goals in the same place where work is being done.

If you lead a team within an organization, among the most important things for you will be ensuring that everyone on the team understands the impact the organization has on the world, how important your group is to the success of the organization as a whole, and how vital the work of each team member is to its success.

6. The creation of an effective process for the selection and adaptation of new employees

Organizational culture begins when someone interacts with your company, such as viewing an ad, calling an HR specialist, showing up for an interview, or going to work for the first time. The success of building a strong, inclusive organizational culture is determined by how comfortable employees feel, how clearly, they understand the processes involved in hiring and onboarding, and how easy it is for them to find the information they need to do their jobs.

Hiring

There are many ways to make hiring processes inclusive and build a strong company culture.

- **Fair pay and reasonable compensation.** Equal pay is a critical component of an inclusive employment system and a healthy culture. It's no secret that there is variation in wages among the various minorities. If you're not already doing so, regularly review your company's key payroll metrics for differentiation by gender and race. As needed, do in-depth equal pay research to ensure that all employees are paid fairly.

- **Teaching hiring managers to control subconscious bias.** Everyone has their subconscious prejudices. It is a mechanism that allows our brain to process information faster. But without timely recognition of unconscious prejudices, they can lead to a distortion of assessment and the perpetuation of stereotypes. To avoid this, organize training for managers and hiring professionals to recognize and combat unconscious biases in the workplace in good time.

- **Refusal of assessment based on conformity to culture.** You can often hear one of the team members say: "I liked them; they fit well into the culture." But such a statement can be misleading. Many people use the term "culture fit" to describe the pleasant feeling of interacting with a potential employee or the positive energy. But the problem is that such feelings are more likely to occur to people similar to us. Cultural fit is essential, but hiring managers need to use precise language when evaluating potential hires. Does the candidate share the values of your organization? Which ones and why? Do they align with your mission? Explain in what way. More specific examples and more precise wording will help to evaluate candidates correctly.

- **You are determining the importance of diversity and inclusion.** Make it clear to all candidates that creating an inclusive culture is a priority for your company. If you haven't already done so, you can add a small commitment statement at the end of the job description.

Adaptation

When you hire a new employee, create an onboarding process that reflects your company culture. Below are a few ways to do this:

- **Communicate to new hires the value of inclusion for your company.** An easy way to help new hires feel included is to emphasize diversity and inclusion during onboarding. New employees will see that your company cares about diversity and inclusion through the onboarding process. This will show them that this is important to your company and their unique qualities.

- **Creation of support and support.** New employees quickly get tired in the first few days of work. One easy way to support them to feel comfortable is by implementing a mentoring system. Introduce newcomers to more experienced colleagues (just not with the authorities) so that they can bring them up to date. The presence of a mentor and the person in charge of the first week of work makes it easier for new employees to ask questions of their coworkers and feel more at ease during that time.

- **Providing new employees with the materials and time they need to succeed is a must.** When creating an inclusive environment, it must be remembered that not everyone perceives information in the same way. If your new hires are participating in onboarding activities, ensure they have access to relevant presentations and information to view them on their own time. In addition, it is necessary to give new employees time and an opportunity to digest all the information about their new job.

Adaptation is a critical moment in ensuring the involvement of employees in the process from the first day they join the company. It sets the tone for a person's interaction with the company, laying the foundation for developing their knowledge and experience while working there. To ensure that your company has a more inclusive culture, you need to ensure that your new employees have a good onboarding experience.

Resistance to Change

When implementing changes and innovations, organizations often have to deal with resistance to change. Why is resistance still a significant barrier to organizational transformation if we know so much, and why do many change agents strive to overcome it?

Change is necessary, and almost every business will have to deal with it. Yet it remains a source of fear for leaders, employees, and customers.

People rarely accept change so quickly. Indeed, resistance to change is an instinct in humans.

In today's world, change is essential to success. This poses a real problem for businesses. Organizations cannot survive if they are slow to innovate and lack professional agility. But inevitably, this means that many people face many changes.

This is why it is essential to know how to deal with resistance in change management.

Change is scary, and it can be hard to live with. It is easier to maintain a well-established habit than to change it. Trying something new involves the risk of failure. Most people would rather stay in their comfort zone than venture into unfamiliar territory.

Even people who claim to enjoy change can find it challenging to navigate the workplace. After all, deciding to change your personal life and accepting organizational change are two very different things. Most often, the source of resistance to change in the workplace is that employees feel no choice. This creates a sense of loss of control and uncertainty. For example, imagine implementing new software across the organization. As a collaborator, you are familiar with the old platform, and you do not necessarily understand the need to introduce a new system. But what you know is that relearning the basic features will require effort. Consciously or unconsciously, you may fear that the change will hurt your job performance.

Too often, employees focus on what they have to lose rather than what they have to gain.

Why Does Resistance Arise?

We have determined what resistance to change is and who is likely to resist change, but we have not identified why this phenomenon occurs.

The first reason, and perhaps the most obvious, is the fear of the unknown and the uncertainty that any change generates. This is a natural human reaction outside of the workplace, but fear of the unknown can mean uncertainty and unpredictability within an organization. As the saying goes, "The best is the enemy of the good," so employees who don't understand the reason for the change will see it as a threat to their job security and, therefore, resist it.

Similarly, the feeling of a loss of control will arouse resistance among employees. If they feel that the current changes are being imposed against their will, they will resist them. By ensuring two-way communication between change managers and employees, you foster a sense of buy-in and let them know that their opinion matters and that they are "kept on the scent."

Conversely, poor communication will lead to resistance to change. If employees don't feel like they are part of the processor aren't kept up to date on the progress of a project, they will either be resistant to change or completely uninterested in it.

None of these reactions are desirable when making changes because you need cooperation at all levels. If the change process is communicated effectively and people understand why the change is happening and how it will improve their daily lives, they won't feel the need to resist it.

Finally, we are all the products of our experiences. If employees have had bad experiences with organizational change, they will project those fears onto the shift taking place. Change managers must be careful and listen to the experiences of their collaborators to ensure that similar mistakes are not repeated. When employees feel their voice counts, they are more receptive to change and less likely to resist it.

The Surprising Benefits of Resistance to Change

Contrary to popular belief, resistance to change is not inherently wrong. It can be a good thing.

First, it forces management to choose their battles carefully. The reluctance of employees raises whether this change will generate significant growth. In other words, is the game worth the candle? This reflection helps ensure that money isn't spent on projects that might not work out.

Second, resistance promotes planning and communication. Management should figure out where resistance is most likely to happen and develop a plan to stop it.

So now that change and resistance to change scare us a little less, let's look at how best to manage people during the implementation of organizational change.

Effective change management is about understanding what underlies resistance to change. From there, you can address the biggest concerns of your employees.

The Best Strategies for Overcoming Unproductive Resistance to Change

Listen First; Speak Later

The first strategy for overcoming resistance to change is communication. Communication is vital. You already know that. However, try to let your collaborators take the initiative in the conversation. People want to be listened to, and by allowing them to express their opinions, you will lessen the frustration they feel about the situation.

In addition, the thoughts, concerns, and suggestions of your employees will prove extremely useful in guiding your change project. At the very least, understanding them will allow you to identify the source of their resistance.

Communicate the Reasons for The Change

The following strategy for overcoming resistance to change is to communicate the why, what, and how. Develop a communication plan beyond telling your employees what you want them to do. Influential communication segments and targets each audience, focusing on what interests them and what they need to know. Emphasize how this change will benefit them.

Be Enthusiastic

How you communicate change has a significant impact on resistance to change. The slightest hesitation will compromise the operation. If you enthusiastically share the reasons for the change, your conviction will be contagious.

Involve Employees

Change is only possible if your human resources are on the same page, so ensure that adaptations are approached from the employees' perspective. If you are implementing a new software system, plan your project with user adoption in mind rather than technology. What matters is not what the technology can do but what the user can accomplish with this new technology.

Delegate the Change

An excellent strategy for overcoming resistance to change is to fight resistance through culture. Prioritize training team members who are natural leaders. They will serve as role models and influencers for the rest of your staff. This creates a ripple effect.

Show Them the Data

Although resistance to change is usually emotional rather than logical, using some hard facts can be an effective complementary strategy. Allow your collaborators to access the data. It's both a great way to demonstrate your transparency and the need for improvement.

Implement Change in Stages

Whether digital or otherwise, no transformation can happen overnight. Good preparation is essential, as are numerous reminders and the participation of employees at all levels. A phased implementation will allow employees to approach change one step at a time, acquiring new skills as they go.

This makes it easier to digest change and makes the task less drastic for those who acquire new skills and gather further information with less resistance to change.

Practice Change Management Exercises

Resistance to change is usually driven by emotions such as fear and the feeling of being endangered. Employees can do many straightforward exercises to simulate the feeling of change to combat this. These drills, which involve bending your arms one way and then swinging them or bouncing balls to show companies they're "bouncing," are also fun and don't induce any sense of danger, unlike a real change. The purpose of these exercises is to show that, although the difference may be uncomfortable at first, you can get used to the new reality reasonably quickly.

An Effective Culture Starts with Commitment

Building an organizational culture takes time and effort, but an influential culture enables employees to do their best.

Such a culture does not arise by itself. You are responsible for its purposeful design, development, and formation.

Remember that employees also shape the culture of the company. When in doubt, take honesty and openness as your allies.

Final Thoughts

The Big Picture

A good dose of inspiration also helps at this time.

After all, in addition to technical and behavioral skills, building successful management can also take place through good examples.

In that sense, we've listed some top leaders in their segments, so you can use encouragement to achieve your goal of being a successful manager.

Check out:

Bill Gates

If you are young and looking to be a successful leader, Bill Gates can be another good source of inspiration.

After all, he started to become one of the most renowned managers globally by founding Microsoft at age 21, alongside Paul Allen.

One of Gates' most famous quotes says a lot about the importance of valuing achievements, but above all, learning from mistakes:

It's okay to celebrate success, but it's more important to heed the lessons of failure.

This is a fundamental leadership principle because a lot can be learned in moments of failure.

Even though he left Microsoft's leadership more than ten years ago, the tech genius continues to exert his leadership through philanthropy.

People who work for the Bill & Melinda Gates Foundation, the world's biggest philanthropic group, work to help people in need and fight for gender equality in the workplace.

Luiza Trajano

Speaking of female empowerment and professional gender equity, how about mentioning a woman who transformed a small chain of stores in So Paulo into one of the world's leading brands?

For over 25 years, Luiza Trajano, the founder of Magazine Luiza, has been an example of entrepreneurial leadership, who for more than 25 decades has stood out in her segment.

Trajano's achievements do not stop there.

When she took her products to the internet in the 1990s, she was one of the first people.

Its virtual store model was copied worldwide, and its efforts are still recognized today.

For a long time, the businesswoman was in charge of Magazine Luiza's SAC to have even closer contact with the public and see how her business could grow even more.

It is never enough to praise female leaders because, despite the many achievements, there is still a substantial historical liability to be repaired.

Steve Jobs

Finally, a leader who has always valued competence, "proposing innovative thoughts," and seeking continuous improvement could not be left out of our list.

Jobs has one characteristic common to all successful leaders for talent and creativity: resilience.

The person who made Apple was known for being able to keep going even when things were going against him, which can be summarized in this quote attributed to him:

"I am convinced that half of what separates successful entrepreneurs from everyone else is sheer perseverance."

Successful leaders do not achieve this status by accident but through dedication.

There is the element of talent, but what counts most at the end of the day is the development of specific skills, a good dose of inspiration, and the search for continuous training.

$$\star\star\star$$

If you enjoyed this title and would like to read about other topics that have changed my life, please check out my new books on Amazon or my website, www.my-mindquide.com.

Also, let's stay connected on social media. Please drop a line on Facebook or Instagram, and stay tuned for updates! You're welcome to share your thoughts with me directly as well: gassner@my-mindquide.com.

In return, I will send you a gorgeous infographic that you can cut out and frame.

Also, please leave a review on Amazon, as this will help me reach an even broader audience. Thank you so much for your time, insight, and undying hunger for knowledge!

I want to say thank you to all my colleagues, clients, friends, and family members, who have all contributed to who I am now.

I also want to thank Gabriel Palacios, a best-selling Swiss author and the king of hypnotherapy. He taught this old fox new tricks, letting me deep-dive into the mystery of hypnotherapy. I learned so much along the journey that I'm now a certified master-hypnosis coach and conversation coach myself!

I also want to thank the great teachers at SAMYANA/Bali who helped me become a yoga and meditation teacher.

Last but not least, I give a special thanks to my master-teacher, Eckhard Wunderle, who is close to a saint to me. He introduced me to the world of meditation and let me discover all the wonders it had to offer. At the Institut für Spirituelle Psychologie, I was able to get my meditation teacher certification from him. I couldn't be prouder.

Peace, love, and happiness to all of you until next time.

References

Larry, W. & Jim, M. (2012). Good Fail, Bad Fail: What Made Caterpillar And Unmade Enron. Retrieved from: https://www.fastcompany.com/3001913/good-fail-bad-fail-what-made-caterpillar-and-unmade-enron

Larry, W. & Jim, M. (2012). Is Your Fear of Failure Holding You Back?. Retrieved from: https://www.cnbc.com/id/49478594

Nasir, K. (2016). Why Failure is Good for Success!. Retrieved from: https://www.lihttps://www.cnbc.com/id/49478594nkedin.com/pulse/why-failure-good-success-nasir-khan

Larry, W. (2011). Leadership Lessons | Learning From Failure. Retrieved from: PeoriaMagazines.com. https://www.peoriamagazines.com/ibi/2011/nov/leadership-lessons

Gary R. Collins, Ph.D. | People Builder's Blog | Page 13. (2013). Adult Education: The Old and the New. Retrieved from: https://peoplebuilder.wordpress.com/author/peoplebuilder/page/13/

Forbes Coaches Council (2021). 15 Pitfalls New C-Suite Leaders Face (And How To Avoid Them). Retrieved from: https://www.forbes.com/sites/forbescoachescouncil/2021/11/30/15-pitfalls-new-c-suite-leaders-face-and-how-to-avoid-them/

Managing across cultures - E-Book. Retrieved from: https://studylib.net/doc/8160100/managing-across-cultures---e-book

Teller report (2021). Jeff Bezos leaves operational controls of Amazon, leaving behind a strong legacy. Retrieved from: https://www.tellerreport.com/news/2021-07-05-jeff-bezos-leaves-operational-controls-of-amazon--leaving-behind-a-strong-legacy---france-24.rJW4MX0gTd.html

Amazon stock Forecast & Predictions for 2021 and Beyond. Retrieved from: https://www.litefinance.com/blog/analysts-opinions/amazon-price-prediction-forecast/

Julian, S. (2021). Elon Musk. Retrieved from: https://saflyer.com/elon-musk/

Hyperloop | transportation project, California, United. Retrieved from: https://www.britannica.com/technology/Hyperloop

Sabrina, M. (2021). Assignment 1.docx - Week 4 Tesla Inc. Retrieved from: https://www.coursehero.com/file/126157348/Assignment-1docx/

Atlantis (2019). Google is 21 years old, all about Google | Made in Atlantis. Retrieved from: https://madeinatlantis.com/2019/10/06/google-is-21-years-old-all-about-google/

Neil, P. (n.d.). All Entrepreneurs Fail: How to Use Failure to Your Advantage. Retrieved from: https://neilpatel.com/blog/entrepreneurs-fail/

Jamie, P. (2019). 10 Reasons Why Startups Fail. Retrieved from: https://www.jamiepride.com/blog/10-reasons-why-startups-fail

Jamie, P. (2018). The ten reasons why startups fail - Dynamic Business. Retrieved from: https://dynamicbusiness.com/topics/start-up-entrepreneur/the-ten-reasons-why-startups-fail.html

Jesse, N. (2021). The Art of Decision-making as an Innovation Leader. Retrieved from: https://www.disruptorleague.com/blog/2021/04/20/the-art-of-decision-making-as-an-innovation-leader/

Samuel, A. (2017). 10 Actions That Will Kill Startup Employee Motivation. Retrieved from: https://www.startups.com/library/expert-advice/11-actions-that-will-kill-your-startups-motivation

Inc Africa (n.d.). 20 Habits of Highly Successful and Effective Leaders. Retrieved from: https://www.inc.com/gordon-tredgold/20-habits-of-highly-successful-and-effective-leaders.html

The Brilliance (2020). 8 Habits Of Successful Leaders You Should Consider. Retrieved from: https://www.thebrilliance.org/habits-of-successful-leaders/

Sherri's, C. (2018). 8 Habits of Highly Successful Leaders - Entrepreneur. Retrieved from: https://www.entrepreneur.com/article/308282

Jeff, H. (2014). 10 Things Only Exceptional Bosses Give Employees. Retrieved from: https://www.linkedin.com/pulse/20140630120036-20017018-10-things-only-exceptional-bosses-give-employees

Matias, R. (2016). Addressing the five negative influences on organizational culture. Retrieved from: https://workplaceinsight.net/addressing-five-negative-influences-organisational-culture/

What are the different types of organizational cultures? Retrieved from: https://tedomidile.weebly.com/uploads/1/3/2/7/132712102/3209c55d78fc0.pdf

Tegra (n.d.). How does a company's growth culture evolve? Retrieved from: https://tegra.co/blog/how-does-a-companys-growth-culture-evolving/

Boris, G., Jeremiah, L., Jesse, P. & J. Yo-Jud, C. (2018). The Leader's Guide to Corporate Culture. Retrieved from: https://hbr.org/2018/01/the-leaders-guide-to-corporate-culture

HR Consultant (2021). Growth culture: find out why to adopt it in the company. Retrieved from: https://hrconsultantuk.co.uk/growth-culture-find-out-why-to-adopt-it-in-the-company/

Chris, S. (2018). Top 6 Strategies to Overcome Resistance to Change. Retrieved from: https://medium.com/@changemblog/top-6-strategies-to-overcome-resistance-to-change-fc458e4f0a8d

Authors portrait

Kurt Friedrich Gassner has worn many hats throughout his lifetime, including but not limited to serial entrepreneur, Creative Director, Meditation Teacher, Licensed Hypnotherapist, and more recently, self-improvement author. Leveraging his treasure trove of experiences and in-depth knowledge of psychology, he provides his readers with the tools they need to unlock their infinite potential.

As a prolific self-help writer, Kurt has authored the following books: *The Art of Forgiveness*, *Lie or Die*, *Soul-Match*, *Can You Inherit a Poisoned Mind?* and *The Power of Poverty*. He also authored a best-selling children's book in German-speaking countries and has over 20 books underway.

When it comes to enduring success, Kurt understands that financial prosperity isn't the only aspect one should strive for. He may be a self-made millionaire, but what really transformed his life is mastering his unconscious mind. Perseverance, personal power, self-awareness, and learning from past mistakes have all been key ingredients to bringing his dreams to fruition—and he strives to impart that wisdom onto others through his writing.

During his spare time, Kurt Friedrich Gassner is either traveling across the globe, golfing, biking in the Alps, hiking, or spending quality time with his loved ones. For the last 37 years, he has been happily married and he is the father of two successful children. Presently, he resides in both Munich, Germany, and Kirchberg, Austria.

OTHER BOOKS BY THE AUTHOR

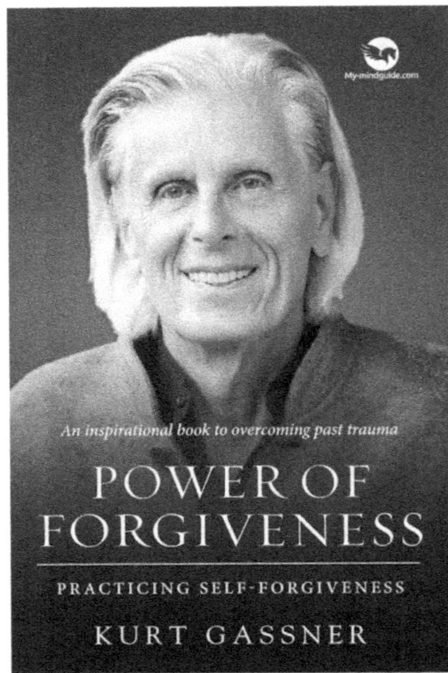

BÜCHER VOM AUTOR IN DEUTSCHER AUSGABE

OTHER BOOKS BY THE AUTHOR

ECKO
FIRED FOR SUCCESS?
TRUE STORIES AND MANAGEMENT LESSONS
FOR OUR TOUGH CHANGING TIMES
KURT GASSNER

ECKO
WEGEN ERFOLG GEFEUERT
Eine wahre Geschichte über das Scheitern in Unternehmen und
was junge Führungskräfte aus einer Fehlerkultur lernen können.
KURT GASSNER

My-mindguide.com
Unlocking
The Healing
Power of Pets
What Pets Can Tell You About Your Soul
KURT GASSNER

My-mindguide.com
Heilkraft
Unserer
Lieblinge
Was Haustiere über Ihre Seele verraten können
KURT GASSNER

My-mindguide.com
THE BLISS OF STRUGGLE
WINNING STRATEGIES FOR DEMANDING TIMES
KURT GASSNER

My-mindguide.com
STARK DURCH „STRUGGLES"
DAS IDEALE MINDSET, UM KRISEN ZU MEISTERN
KURT GASSNER

My-mindguide.com
LIE LYING & LIAR
A LIE HAS NO LEGS BUT IT HAS WINGS
KURT GASSNER

My-mindguide.com
LÜGE LÜGEN & LÜGNER
EINE LÜGE HAT KEINE BEINE, ABER SIE HAT FLÜGEL
KURT GASSNER

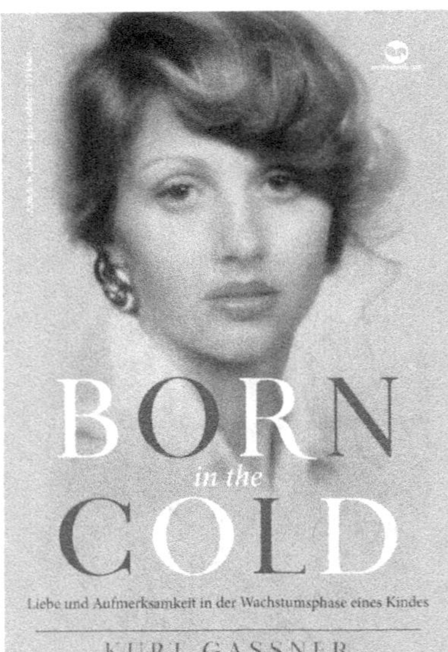

BORN
in the
COLD
Liebe und Aufmerksamkeit in der Wachstumsphase eines Kindes
KURT GASSNER

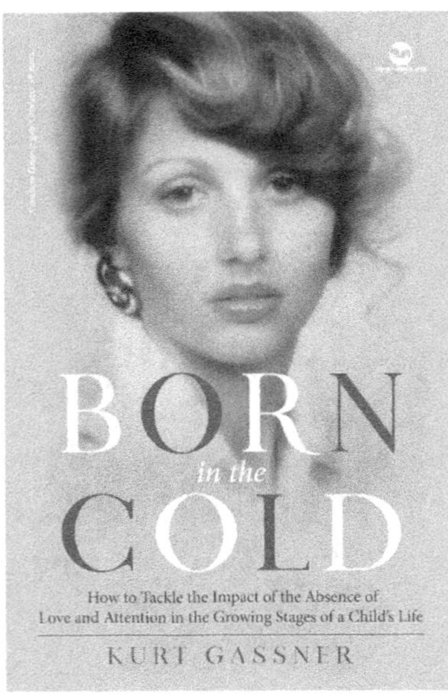

BORN
in the
COLD
How to Tackle the Impact of the Absence of
Love and Attention in the Growing Stages of a Child's Life
KURT GASSNER

SOPHIAS WUNDERWELT
10 ERZÄHLUNGEN
KURT GASSNER

SOPHIA'S WONDERWORLD
10 TALES
KURT GASSNER

BESTSELLING AUTHOR OF
The Art Of
FORGIVNESS
AMAZON #1 BESTSELLER
My-mindguide.com
A practical guide for self healing and overcome past traumas
The Art Of
FORGIVNESS
KURT GASSNER
The Art Of
FORGIVNESS
KURT GASSNER

www.ingramcontent.com/pod-product-compliance
Lightning Source LLC
LaVergne TN
LVHW041308200726
843509LV00009B/418